GCSE
Success

Maths

Foundation Tier

Revision Guide

**Deborah Dobson,
Phil Duxbury,
Mike Fawcett and
Aftab Ilahi**

Contents

GEOMETRY AND MEASURES

PROBABILITY

STATISTICS

Contents 3

Adding and subtracting integers

Adding a **negative** number **or** subtracting a **positive** number will have the **same result**.

$$3 + -5 = -2$$
$$3 - +5 = -2$$

Go down by 5.

Use a **number line** to visualise the answer.

Adding a **negative** number means subtract.

Subtracting a **negative** number means add.

Adding a positive number **or** subtracting a negative number will have the **same result**.

$$-1 + +4 = +3$$
$$-1 - -4 = +3$$

Go up by 4.

+ +	means	+
+ –	means	–
– +	means	–
– –	means	+

Multiplying and dividing integers

Look at these examples.

Multiplying a negative number by a positive number always gives a negative answer.

$$-5 \times +3 = -15$$
$$+5 \times -3 = -15$$

Multiplying two positive numbers **or** multiplying two negative numbers always gives a positive answer.

$$+4 \times +3 = +12$$
$$-4 \times -3 = +12$$

The same rules work for division.

$$+10 \div -5 = -2$$
$$-10 \div -5 = +2$$

This table summarises the rules:

+	× or ÷	+	=	+
+	× or ÷	–	=	–
–	× or ÷	+	=	–
–	× or ÷	–	=	+

A positive number multiplied by a negative number gives a negative answer.

A negative number multiplied by a negative number gives a positive answer.

KEYWORDS

Integer ➤ An integer is a whole number; it can be positive, negative or zero.

Positive ➤ A number above zero.

Negative ➤ A number below zero.

Place Value and Ordering

Module 1

Use of symbols

Look at the following symbols and their meanings.

Symbol	Meaning	Examples
>	Greater than	5 > 3 (5 is greater than 3)
<	Less than	−4 < −1 (−4 is less than −1)
≥	Greater than or equal to	$x \geq 2$ (x can be 2 or higher)
≤	Less than or equal to	$x \leq -3$ (x can be −3 or lower)
=	Equal to	2 + +3 = 2 − −3
≠	Not equal to	$4^2 \neq 4 \times 2$ (16 is not equal to 8)

Place value

Look at this example.

Given that 23 × 47 = 1081, work out 2.3 × 4.7

The answer to 2.3 × 4.7 must have the digits 1 0 8 1 ← Do a quick estimate to find where the decimal point goes.

2.3 is about 2 and 4.7 is about 5. Since 2 × 5 = 10, the answer must be about 10.

Therefore 2.3 × 4.7 = 10.81

Write the following symbols and numbers on separate pieces of paper.

| + | − | × | ÷ | = | 0 |

| +2 | −2 | +4 | −4 | +8 | −8 |

Arrange them to form a correct calculation.

How many different calculations can you make? For example:

| +2 | − | −2 | = | +4 |

---

1. Calculate the following:
   (a) −5 − −8
   (b) −2 + −6
   (c) −7 + −3 − −5
2. Calculate the following:
   (a) −12 × −4
   (b) 24 ÷ −3
   (c) −3 × −4 × −5
3. State whether these statements are true or false.
   (a) 6 < 3
   (b) −4 > −5
   (c) 2 + −3 = 2 − +3
4. Given that 43 × 57 = 2451, calculate the following:
   (a) 4.3 × 0.57
   (b) 430 × 570
   (c) 2451 ÷ 5.7

Highest common factor

The highest common factor (HCF) is the highest **factor** shared by two or more numbers.

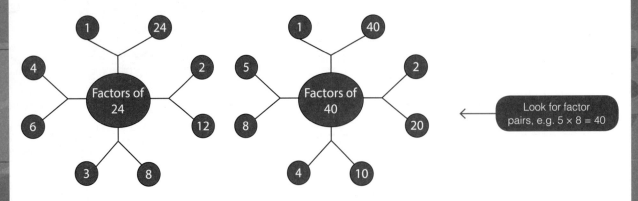

The factors of 24 are 1, 2, 3, 4, 6, (8), 12 and 24.

The factors of 40 are 1, 2, 4, 5, (8), 10, 20 and 40.

Remember – every number has 1 and itself as a factor.

8 is the HCF of 24 and 40.

Lowest common multiple

The lowest common multiple (LCM) is the lowest **multiple** shared by two or more numbers.

The first seven multiples of 5 are: 5, 10, 15, 20, 25, (30), 35, …

The first seven multiples of 6 are: 6, 12, 18, 24, (30), 36, 42, …

The first multiple of any number is itself.

30 is the LCM of 5 and 6.

Prime factors

Numbers can be expressed as the **product** of their **prime factors**. The product of the prime factors can be shown in **index form** where appropriate.

Write 24 as a product of its prime factors.

Use a factor tree to help. Start with the smallest **prime** number that divides exactly into 24 and continue in order until 1 is reached.

Prime numbers: 2, 3, 5, 7, 11, 13, … (1 is not a prime number).

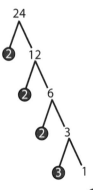

$24 = 2 \times 2 \times 2 \times 3$ ← In index form: $24 = 2^3 \times 3$

Module 2

Factors, Multiples and Primes

HCF and LCM using prime factors

You can find the HCF of two numbers by multiplying their shared prime factors.

You can find the LCM of the two numbers by multiplying the HCF with the rest of the prime factors.

Find the HCF and LCM of 24 and 42.

$24 = 2 \times 2 \times (2 \times 3)$

$42 = (2 \times 3) \times 7$

This can be presented in a Venn diagram.

2×2

2×3

7

Prime factors of 24

Prime factors of 42

HCF

The **HCF** of 24 and 42 = 2×3 = **6**

The LCM of 24 and 42 = 6 × the rest of the prime factors

The **LCM** = $6 \times 2 \times 2 \times 7$ = **168**

Write the following prime numbers on separate pieces of paper.

| 2 | 2 | 3 | 3 | 5 | 7 |

Draw a Venn diagram on a piece of paper and place the prime numbers anywhere in the diagram (at least one in each of the three sections).

Find the product of each of the sections. You will now have two numbers and the HCF of those numbers. Find the LCM of your two numbers.

Repeat by rearranging your prime factors.

1. **(a)** Find all the factors of 12 and 15.
   (b) Find the HCF of 12 and 15.
2. **(a)** List the first 8 multiples of 7 and 5.
   (b) Find the LCM of 7 and 5.
3. Answer these.
   (a) Write the following numbers as a product of their prime factors: 28 and 98.
   (b) Write your answers to part (a) in index form.
   (c) Find the HCF and the LCM of 28 and 98.

Using Bidmas

Bidmas helps you to remember the correct order of a calculation.

Brackets

Indices

Division

Multiplication

Addition

Subtraction

> Start with brackets and then follow this order. Remember that multiplying and dividing comes before adding and subtracting.

Calculate $4 + 3 \times 6$ ← Multiply first and then add.

$4 + 18 = 22$

Remember that brackets followed by indices or **powers** come before any of the four operations.

Calculate $56 - 3^2(4 + 2)$

$56 - 3^2(6)$ ← Brackets

$56 - 9 \times 6$ ← Powers

$56 - 54 = 2$ ← Multiplication then subtraction

In the next example you must calculate the **numerator** and the **denominator** separately before dividing.

$$\frac{8 + 6}{(8 - 3) \times 20} = \frac{14}{5 \times 20} = \frac{14}{100} = 0.14$$

Reciprocals

The **reciprocal** of n is $1 \div n$ or $\frac{1}{n}$

Therefore the reciprocal of 5 is $1 \div 5$ or $\frac{1}{5}$

The reciprocal of $\frac{2}{3}$ is $1 \div \frac{2}{3} = 1 \times \frac{3}{2} = \frac{3}{2}$

> To find the reciprocal you can simply turn the fraction upside down.

KEYWORDS

Powers ➤ Numbers with indices.

Numerator ➤ The top part of a fraction.

Denominator ➤ The bottom part of a fraction.

Reciprocal ➤ The reciprocal of a fraction is obtained by interchanging the numerator and denominator.

Adding and subtracting fractions

You can only add or subtract fractions which have a common denominator.

$\frac{1}{5} + \frac{3}{5} = \frac{1 + 3}{5} = \frac{4}{5}$ ← Keep the denominator the same.

If the denominators are different then find equivalent fractions with the same denominator.

$\frac{2}{3} - \frac{1}{4}$ ← The LCM of 3 and 4 is 12.

× by 4   × by 3

$\frac{8}{12} - \frac{3}{12}$ $= \frac{8 - 3}{12} = \frac{5}{12}$ ← Subtract as normal.

Multiplying and dividing fractions

When multiplying fractions, simply multiply the numerators and then multiply the denominators.

$$\frac{2}{3} \times \frac{3}{5} = \frac{2 \times 3}{3 \times 5} = \frac{6}{15} = \frac{2}{5}$$ ← Don't forget to simplify.

When dividing fractions, you don't actually divide at all. Find the reciprocal of the second fraction and then multiply instead.

multiply instead of divide

$$\frac{2}{3} \div \frac{4}{5} = \frac{2}{3} \times \frac{5}{4} = \frac{2 \times 5}{3 \times 4} = \frac{10}{12} = \frac{5}{6}$$

reciprocal of 2nd fraction

$$\frac{2}{3} \div \frac{4}{5} = \frac{5}{6}$$

Calculating with mixed numbers

When multiplying or dividing with mixed numbers, it's best to convert them to improper fractions.

$$2\frac{1}{4} \times 1\frac{2}{3} = \frac{9}{4} \times \frac{5}{3} = \frac{9 \times 5}{4 \times 3} = \frac{45}{12} = \frac{15}{4} = 3\frac{3}{4}$$

change to improper fractions

$$2\frac{1}{4} \times 1\frac{2}{3} = 3\frac{3}{4}$$

When adding or subtracting mixed numbers, you should deal with the fraction part separately.

$$2\frac{1}{4} \quad + \quad 3\frac{1}{3}$$

$$2 + 3 = 5 \qquad \frac{1}{4} + \frac{1}{3} = \frac{3}{12} + \frac{4}{12} = \frac{7}{12}$$

$$2\frac{1}{4} + 3\frac{1}{3} = 5\frac{7}{12}$$

Fold a piece of A4 paper in half three times. Open it out and shade $\frac{3}{8}$ of it.

Fold the paper back in half five times. Open it out and shade in $\frac{9}{32}$ (make sure you shade nine unshaded areas).

Count the total number of shaded squares to find the answer to $\frac{3}{8} + \frac{9}{32}$.

1. Calculate the following:
   (a) $6 + 3 \times 4$
   (b) $(7 - 4) \times (6 + 2)$
   (c) $(3 + 4^2) \times 2$
   (d) $\dfrac{5^2 + 3}{2 \times \sqrt{49}}$

2. Find the reciprocal of:
   (a) $\frac{2}{5}$
   (b) $\frac{1}{7}$
   (c) 5
   (d) 0.25

3. Work out:
   (a) $\frac{4}{5} - \frac{3}{4}$
   (b) $2\frac{1}{4} + 3\frac{3}{8}$
   (c) $\frac{4}{7} \div \frac{0}{5}$
   (d) $2\frac{2}{3} \times 1\frac{3}{4}$

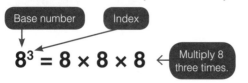

Index form and roots

The index number tells you how many times the base number is multiplied.

Base number   Index

$$8^3 = 8 \times 8 \times 8 \leftarrow \text{Multiply 8 three times.}$$

Base number   Index

$$4^5 = 4 \times 4 \times 4 \times 4 \times 4 \leftarrow \text{Multiply 4 five times.}$$

The following table shows you how to calculate **roots**.

Roots	How to say it	Reasoning
$\sqrt{25} = 5$	Square root of 25 equals 5	Because $5 \times 5 = 25$
$\sqrt[3]{8} = 2$	Cube root of 8 equals 2	Because $2 \times 2 \times 2 = 8$
$\sqrt[4]{81} = 3$	Fourth root of 81 equals 3	Because $3 \times 3 \times 3 \times 3 = 81$
$\sqrt[5]{32} = 2$	Fifth root of 32 equals 2	Because $2 \times 2 \times 2 \times 2 \times 2 = 32$

4

Index laws

$\leftarrow$ Index laws only apply when the base numbers are the same.

Multiplying $\longrightarrow$ Add powers to give final index.

$$4^2 \times 4^3 = 4^{2+3} = 4^5 \qquad\qquad a^2 \times a^{-3} \times a^6 = a^{2-3+6} = a^5 \leftarrow \text{Normal rules apply for negative numbers.}$$

Dividing $\longrightarrow$ Subtract powers to give final index.

$$5^7 \div 5^3 = 5^{7-3} = 5^4 \qquad\qquad b^9 \div b = b^{9-1} = b^8 \leftarrow \text{If no power is given, assume it is 1.}$$

Raising one power to another power $\longrightarrow$ Multiply powers to give final index.

$$(3^2)^4 = 3^{2 \times 4} = 3^8 \qquad\qquad (c^2)^{-3} = c^{2 \times -3} = c^{-6} \quad \boxed{\text{Also see page 21.}}$$

Zero and negative indices

These rules can be used to **evaluate** more difficult indices.

Rule	Example
$x^0 = 1$	$5^0 = 1$
$x^{-n} = \dfrac{1}{x^n}$	$6^{-2} = \dfrac{1}{6^2} = \dfrac{1}{36}$

$\leftarrow$ Any non-zero number raised to the power of 0 equals 1.

$\leftarrow$ Write down the reciprocal and change the sign of the index.

Fold a piece of paper in half six times and measure its thickness.

If it were possible, how many times would you need to fold it until it was thicker than 30cm? Or taller than your house? Or taller than the Eiffel Tower?

Open the piece of paper which was folded six times and count the rectangles. Consider why the total number of rectangles is $2^6 = 64$.

Powers and Roots

Module 4

Standard form

Standard form is a useful way of writing very large or very small numbers using powers of 10.
A number written in standard form looks like this:

$A \times 10^n$ ← A power of 10 where n is an integer.

A is between 1 and 10 (not including 10).

Look at this example to write very large numbers in standard form:

$5\,000\,000 = 5 \times 1\,000\,000$ ← 1 million = 10^6

$\qquad\qquad = 5 \times 10^6$

This is 5 000 000 in standard form.

$43\,000\,000$ is written as 4.3×10^7

Use all the non-zero digits.

Count all the digits after the 4 (1 + 6 = 7).

Look at this example to write numbers less than 1 in standard form:

$0.00007 = 7 \div 100\,000$

$\qquad\quad = 7 \div 10^5$

$\qquad\quad = 7 \times 10^{-5}$

Index number is always negative for these types.

0.000638 is written as 6.38×10^{-4} ← The digits have moved four decimal places.

Know the following powers of 10:

$1000 = 10^3$

$100 = 10^2$

$10 = 10^1$

$1 = 10^0$

$0.1 = 10^{-1}$

$0.01 = 10^{-2}$

$0.001 = 10^{-3}$

Calculating with standard form

When multiplying or dividing, deal with the powers separately.

$(4 \times 10^6) \times (8 \times 10^{-3}) = (4 \times 8) \times (10^6 \times 10^{-3}) = 32 \times 10^3$

Remember to put your answer back into standard form → $= 3.2 \times 10^4$

$(5 \times 10^7) \div (2 \times 10^6) = \dfrac{5 \times 10^7}{2 \times 10^6}$

$\qquad\qquad\qquad\qquad = \dfrac{5}{2} \times \dfrac{10^7}{10^6}$

$\qquad\qquad\qquad\qquad = 2.5 \times 10^1$ ← Subtract indices when dividing.

When adding or subtracting, convert the values to ordinary numbers first.

$(5 \times 10^5) - (4 \times 10^4) = 500\,000 - 40\,000 = 460\,000$

$\qquad\qquad\qquad\qquad\qquad\qquad = 4.6 \times 10^5$

$(3.2 \times 10^{-3}) + (4.3 \times 10^{-4}) = 0.0032 + 0.00043$

$\qquad\qquad\qquad\qquad\qquad = 0.00363$

$\qquad\qquad\qquad\qquad\qquad = 3.63 \times 10^{-3}$

1. Write the following in index form.
    (a) $4 \times 4 \times 4$
    (b) $3 \times 3 \times 3 \times 3 \times 3$
    (c) $\dfrac{1}{2 \times 2 \times 2}$

2. (a) Simplify the following, leaving your answer in index form.
    (i) $3^4 \times 3^5$ (ii) $4^8 \div 4$
    (iii) $\dfrac{6^2 \times 6^8}{6^3}$
    (b) Evaluate the following.
    (i) 7^0 (ii) 5^{-3}
    (iii) $\sqrt[4]{16}$

3. (a) Write the following in standard form.
    (i) 6000   (ii) 2300
    (iii) 0.00678   (iv) 0.15
    (b) Calculate the following, leaving your answer in standard form.
    (i) $(3 \times 10^4) \times (6 \times 10^5)$
    (ii) $(8 \times 10^0) \div (4 \times 10^5)$
    (iii) $(5.1 \times 10^6) - (3.9 \times 10^5)$

Converting between fractions, decimals and percentages

Make sure you know these key fraction, percentage and decimal equivalences.

Fraction	Decimal	Percentage
$\frac{1}{3}$	0.333…	$33\frac{1}{3}\%$
$\frac{1}{4}$	0.25	25%
$\frac{2}{5}$	0.4	40%
$\frac{3}{10}$	0.3	30%
$\frac{5}{100}$	0.05	5%
$\frac{75}{100}$	0.75	75%
$\frac{3}{8}$	0.375	$37\frac{1}{2}\%$

$1 \div 4 = 0.25, 0.25 \times 100 = 25\%$

5

Fractions to decimals

Convert simple fractions into decimals by division.

$\frac{5}{8} = 5 \div 8 = 0.625$

$$8\overline{)5.\,{}^50\,{}^20\,{}^40} = 0.\,6\,2\,5$$

Use a written method if no calculator.

Another simple way of converting fractions into decimals is by finding an equivalent fraction with a denominator of 100.

$\frac{7}{20}$ is equivalent to $\frac{35}{100} = 0.35$ ← Multiply the numerator and denominator by 5.

$\frac{21}{25}$ is equivalent to $\frac{84}{100} = 0.84$ ← Multiply the numerator and denominator by 4.

Therefore $\frac{7}{20} = 0.35$ and $\frac{21}{25} = 0.84$

When ordering a mixture of fractions, decimals and percentages, convert all the values to the same type (e.g. all into decimals).

Write the following in order, from smallest to largest: $\frac{2}{5}$, $\frac{1}{4}$, 0.3, 28%

$\frac{2}{5} = 0.4$, $\frac{1}{4} = 0.25$ and 28% = 0.28

So $\frac{1}{4}$, 28%, 0.3, $\frac{2}{5}$ is the correct order.

Terminating decimals to fractions

A **terminating decimal** is a decimal number where the digits after the decimal point do not go on forever, e.g. 0.2, 0.35 and 0.875.

Convert decimals into fractions using $\frac{1}{10}$, $\frac{1}{100}$ and $\frac{1}{1000}$, etc.

$0.8 = \frac{8}{10} = \frac{4}{5}$

$0.48 = \frac{48}{100} = \frac{12}{25}$ — Use HCF to cancel fractions to their simplest form.

$0.134 = \frac{134}{1000} = \frac{67}{500}$

Multiplying by a decimal

It is best to ignore the decimals and multiply the whole numbers using a written method.

Look at these examples.

4.2×3.8

40	2	
1200	60	30
320	16	8

```
    1 2 0 0
      3 2 0
        6 0
  +     1 6
    1 5 9 6
```

$42 \times 38 = 1596$

$4.2 \times 3.8 = 15.96$ ← A quick estimate will help place the decimal point ($4.2 \times 3.8 \approx 4 \times 4 = 16$)

2.23×4.9

200	20	3	
8000	800	120	40
1800	180	27	9

```
        2 2 3
  ×       4 9
      2 0 0 7
      8 9 2 0
    1 0 9 2 7
```

$223 \times 49 = 10\,927$

$2.23 \times 4.9 = 10.927$ ← A quick estimate will help place the decimal point ($2.23 \times 4.9 \approx 2 \times 5 = 10$)

KEYWORDS

Terminating decimal ➤ A decimal number in which the digits do not repeat continuously.

Divisor ➤ The number which you are dividing by.

Adding and subtracting decimals

Use a column method to add or subtract decimals, e.g. $4.3 - 2.82$

```
  ³4 . ¹²3 ¹0     ← Place a zero in the
  - 2 . 8  2         hundredths column.
    1 . 4  8
```

Dividing by a decimal

It is best to change the **divisor** to a whole number.

$45 \div 0.3 = 450 \div 3 = 150$ ← Multiplying both numbers by 10 gives the exact same calculation.

$1.23 \div 0.15 = 123 \div 15 = 8.2$ ← Multiply both numbers by 100.

Draw a 5 × 5 grid onto squared paper. Shade $\frac{7}{25}$ of the grid.

Draw an extra line in the centre of every row and column to turn it into a 10 × 10 grid.

Count the shaded squares to find out what $\frac{7}{25}$ is as a percentage and a decimal.

1. Convert the following fractions to decimals.
   (a) $\frac{3}{5}$ (b) $\frac{7}{8}$ (c) $\frac{2}{3}$ (d) $\frac{13}{20}$

2. Convert the following decimals to fractions.
   (a) 0.36 (b) 0.248 (c) 0.08

3. Without a calculator, work out:
   (a) 6.3×4.9 (b) $12 \div 0.4$ (c) $7.2 \div 0.5$

Rounding

When rounding you must always look at the digit in the next column:

If it is 5 or more, you round up.

Example	Nearest whole	Nearest ten
382.5	383	380
86.4	86	90
59.7	60	60

If it is 4 or less, you round down.

Example	Nearest hundred	Nearest thousand
6482	6500	6000
3549	3500	4000
10859	10900	11000

Decimal places

It is important to give an answer to an appropriate **degree of accuracy**. Remember that you should never round a number until you have the final answer of a calculation.

Units	Usual degree of accuracy
Centimetres (cm)	1 decimal place
Metres (m)	2 decimal places
Kilometres (km)	3 decimal places

> Rounding to two decimal places (2 d.p.) will leave you with two digits after the decimal point.

Round 3.476 32 to 2 d.p.

> Round up since the next digit on the right is 5 or more.

3 . 4 7|6 3 2 = 3 . 4 8 (to 2 d.p.)

> Round after the second digit.

> Look at the next digit on the right.

Round 2.459 73 to 3 d.p.

> Since the fourth digit is a 7 and the third digit is a 9, round the second digit up by 1.

2 . 4 5 9|7 3 = 2 . 4 6 0 (to 3 d.p.)

> Round after the third digit.

Significant figures

Rounding to significant figures (s.f.) is useful for very large and very small numbers. The first significant figure of any number is the first digit which is not zero.

2 4 0 3 2 0   0 . 0 2 4 0 3 2 0

> The next digits (4, 0, 3 etc.) on the right are the second, third, fourth (etc.) significant figures.

> First s.f.

Example	1 s.f.	2 s.f.	3 s.f.
40857	40000	41000	40900
0.004592	0.005	0.0046	0.00459
12.93	10	13	12.9
1.987	2	2.0	1.99

KEYWORDS

Degree of accuracy ➤ What a number has been rounded to.

Upper bound ➤ The highest possible limit.

Lower bound ➤ The lowest possible limit.

Estimation

It is important to have an approximate idea of an answer before starting any calculation.
To estimate a calculation, it is best to round each number to 1 significant figure.

Estimate $\dfrac{3.4 \times 37}{0.21}$

$\dfrac{3.4 \times 37}{0.21} \approx \dfrac{3 \times 40}{0.2} = \dfrac{120}{0.2}$

Multiply the numerator and the denominator by 10.

$$= \dfrac{1200}{2} = 600$$

Estimate, to 1 significant figure, the total cost for 391 pupils to go on a school trip which costs £23 per person.

$391 \times 23 \approx 400 \times 20 = £8000$

Use a tape measure to find the length and width of your bedroom to the nearest centimetre.

What are the limits of accuracy for the length and width of your bedroom?

Limits of accuracy

When a measurement is taken, it is usually rounded to an appropriate degree of accuracy. The limits of accuracy are the maximum and minimum possible values for the measurement:

➤ The **upper bound** is the maximum possible value the measurement could have been.
➤ The **lower bound** is the minimum possible value the measurement could have been.

The bounds are exactly half the degree of accuracy above and below the measurement.

You can write the limits of accuracy using inequalities as shown.

Measurement	Degree of accuracy	Lower bound	Upper bound	Limits of accuracy
23mm	Nearest mm	22.5mm	23.5mm	$22.5 \leqslant x < 23.5$
54.6cm	1 decimal place	54.55cm	54.65cm	$54.55 \leqslant x < 54.65$
4.32m	2 decimal places	4.315m	4.325m	$4.315 \leqslant x < 4.325$
34 000km	2 significant figures	33 500km	34 500km	$33 500 \leqslant x < 34 500$

Upper bound is actually 23.499…

We use the < symbol to mean 'up to but not including' 23.5

1. Round the following.
   (a) 38.4 to the nearest whole number
   (b) 365 to the nearest ten
   (c) 439 to the nearest hundred
   (d) 4505 to the nearest thousand
2. Round the following.
   (a) 2.3874 to 2 d.p.   (b) 4.609 92 to 3 d.p.
   (c) 43 549 to 2 s.f.   (d) 0.004 034 9 to 3 s.f.

3. Estimate $\dfrac{28 \times 4.9}{0.18}$

4. Write down, using inequalities, the limits of accuracy of the following measurements which have been rounded to the accuracy stated.
   (a) 23m (nearest m)   (b) 4.7kg (1 d.p.)
   (c) 5.23km (3 s.f.)

Calculator buttons

On a scientific calculator there are several buttons which are essential to know.

The table shows the button and its use. ← Some calculators are different, so make sure you know how to use yours.

Button	Use	Example
x^2	**Square**	$16^2 \longrightarrow$ 16 x^2 = $\longrightarrow$ 256
x^3	**Cube**	$7^3 \longrightarrow$ 7 x^3 = $\longrightarrow$ 343
y^x	Power	$3^6 \longrightarrow$ 3 y^x 6 = $\longrightarrow$ 729
$\sqrt{}$	Square root	$\sqrt{60} \longrightarrow$ $\sqrt{}$ 60 = $\longrightarrow$ 7.75 (to 2 d.p.)
$\sqrt[3]{}$	Cube root	$\sqrt[3]{125} \longrightarrow$ 2nd F $\sqrt[3]{}$ 125 = $\longrightarrow$ 5
$\sqrt[x]{}$	xth root	$\sqrt[5]{32} \longrightarrow$ 5 2nd F $\sqrt[x]{}$ 32 = $\longrightarrow$ 2
$a\frac{b}{c}$	Fraction	$\frac{8}{5} \longrightarrow$ 8 $a\frac{b}{c}$ 5 = $\longrightarrow$ $1\frac{3}{5}$ ← Some calculators use the button ▢
$\times10^x$	Standard form	$3.4 \times 10^4 \longrightarrow$ 3.4 $\times10^x$ 4 = $\longrightarrow$ 34 000 ← Some calculators use the button Exp

Using brackets

Typing a large calculation into a calculator will usually require the use of brackets.

Calculate $\dfrac{23 + 4.5^2}{6.9 - 2.3}$

Type (23 + 4.5 x^2) ÷ (6.9 − 2.3) = 9.402 173 913 ← Do not round off unless directed to do so.

It can be beneficial to do a check by calculating the numerator and denominator separately.

$\dfrac{23 + 4.5^2}{6.9 - 2.3} = \dfrac{43.25}{4.6}$ ← Show this working in an exam.

$= 9.402\,173\,913$

7

Standard form

Standard form calculations can be performed on a calculator. However, brackets are essential to separate the numbers.

Calculate $(2.1 \times 10^3) \times (4.5 \times 10^8)$

Type (2.1 ×10ˣ 3) × (4.5 ×10ˣ 8) = 9.45×10^{11} ← The calculator will display this answer in standard form.

Use the (−) button for negative indices.

Calculate $(3.6 \times 10^4) \div (2.5 \times 10^{-3})$

Type (3.6 ×10ˣ 4) ÷ (2.5 ×10ˣ (−) 3) = 14 400 000

$$= 1.44 \times 10^7$$ ← Change the answer back into standard form if required.

Make the number 16 by using the following calculator buttons.

| 3 | 4 | 5 | (|) | $\sqrt[3]{\ }$ | y^x | + | = |

You must only use each button once.

---

1. Calculate the following.
   (a) 2.3^3
   (b) 4^6
   (c) $\sqrt[3]{512}$

2. Calculate the following. Write down all the figures on your calculator display.
   $$\frac{8 + 2.5^2}{\sqrt{20.25}}$$

3. Calculate the following. Give your answer in standard form to 3 s.f.
   (a) $(2.6 \times 10^5) \times (3.8 \times 10^{-2})$
   (b) $(4.7 \times 10^8) \div (6.3 \times 10^{-7})$

Squares, cubes and roots

Index laws

Index notation

Mixed numbers

Reciprocals

Powers

Standard form

Prime factors

Highest common factor

Integers

Calculators

Lowest common multiple

Improper

Fractions

Number

Negatives

Percentages

Bidmas

Four operations

Approximations

Estimation

Significant figures

Decimals

Rounding

Place value

Decimal places

Limits of accuracy

1. Work out the following. ⊚

   (a) 4×5.8 **[2]**   **(b)** 2.3×42.7 **[3]**

   (c) $24 \div 0.08$ **[2]**   **(d)** $46.8 \div 3.6$ **[2]**

   (e) $-3 + -4$ **[1]**   **(f)** $-2 - -5 + -6$ **[1]**

   (g) $45 \div -9$ **[1]**   **(h)** $-4 \times -5 \times -7$ **[1]**

   (i) $4 + 3^2 \times 7$ **[1]**   **(j)** $(5 - 6^2) - (4 + \sqrt{25})$ **[2]**

2. **(a)** Write 36 as a product of its prime factors. Write your answer in index form. ⊚ **[2]**

   (b) Write 48 as a product of its prime factors. Write your answer in index form. ⊚ **[2]**

   (c) Find the highest common factor of 48 and 36. ⊚ **[2]**

   (d) Find the lowest common multiple of 48 and 36. ⊚ **[2]**

3. **(a)** Work out the following.

   $$\frac{4}{3} \times \frac{5}{6}$$

   Write your answer as a mixed number in its simplest form. ⊚ **[2]**

   (b) The sum of three mixed numbers is $7\frac{11}{12}$. Two of the numbers are $2\frac{3}{4}$ and $3\frac{5}{6}$.

   Find the third number and give your answer in its simplest form. ⊚ **[3]**

   (c) Calculate $3\frac{1}{5} \div 2\frac{1}{4}$

   Give your answer as a mixed number in its simplest form. ⊚ **[3]**

4. Simplify the following, leaving your answer in index form. ⊚

   (a) $5^3 \div 5^{-5}$ **[1]**   **(b)** $3^4 \times 3^8 \times 3$ **[1]**   **(c)** $\dfrac{7^2 \times 7^5}{7^3}$ **[2]**

5. Calculate the value of the following. ⊚

   (a) 2.3^0 **[1]**   **(b)** 5^4 **[1]**   **(c)** 3^{-2} **[2]**

6. **(a)** Write the following numbers in standard form. ⊚

   (i) 67 000 000 **[1]**   **(ii)** 0.000 007 **[1]**

   (iii) 43 600 **[1]**   **(iv)** 0.008 03 **[1]**

   (b) Calculate the following, giving your answers in standard form. ⊚

   (i) $(4 \times 10^6) \times (3 \times 10^5)$ **[2]**

   (ii) $(2.1 \times 10^{-2}) + (5.7 \times 10^{-3})$ **[2]**

   (iii) $(1.2 \times 10^8) \div (3 \times 10^4)$ **[2]**

7. Paul's garage measures 6m in length to the nearest metre. His new car measures 5.5m in length to 1 decimal place.

   Write down, using inequalities, the limits of accuracy of:

   (a) Paul's garage   **[2]**

   (b) Paul's new car   **[2]**

Letters multiplied together

Make sure you know these rules:

a^3 means $a \times a \times a$ ← But $3a$ means $a + a + a$.

pq^3 means $p \times q \times q \times q$ ← You only cube the q.

$4x^2$ means $4 \times x \times x$ ← You only square the x.

$(pq)^3$ means $p \times q \times p \times q \times p \times q$

$\dfrac{p}{q}$ means $p \div q$

Terms

Algebraic **terms** are separated by + and – signs.
A **coefficient** is a number or letter multiplying a term.

The coefficient of x is 3.

The coefficient of x^2y is $\dfrac{2}{5}$

$$3x - 4y + \frac{2}{5}x^2y$$

This term could be written as $0.4x^2y$ but it is more usual to use fractions as coefficients.

The coefficient of y is –4.

Simplifying expressions

An **expression** is a collection of (one or more) algebraic terms. 'Like terms' have the same combination of letters. Here is an example of an expression:

$9p$ and $-6p$ are like terms. They can be collected to give $3p$.

$$9p + 3pq + 5pq - 6p$$

$3pq$ and $5pq$ are like terms. They can be collected to give $8pq$.

So $9p + 3pq + 5pq - 6p = 3p + 8pq$

Combinations of letters that are **not** the same are said to be **unlike** terms.
For example, $2xy$ and xy^2 are unlike terms. They can't be added together.

KEYWORDS

Term ➤ A single number or variable, or numbers and variables multiplied together.

Coefficient ➤ The number occurring at the start of each term.

Expression ➤ A collection of terms.

Indices (powers) ➤ A convenient way of writing repetitive multiplication, e.g. $3^4 = 3 \times 3 \times 3 \times 3 = 81$. In this example, the power of 3 is 4.

Identity ➤ An equation that is true for all values.

Module 8
Algebraic Notation

Laws of indices

Make sure you know these seven rules:

Rule in words	Rule in symbols	Examples
When multiplying numbers with the same base, you add the **indices**	$a^m \times a^n = a^{m+n}$	$p^4 \times p^3 = p^{(4+3)} = p^7$ $2^7 \times 2^3 = 2^{10}$
When dividing numbers with the same base, you subtract the indices	$a^m \div a^n = a^{m-n}$	$q^8 \div q^3 = q^{(8-3)} = q^5$ $3^{13} \div 3^8 = 3^5$
When finding a power of a power, you multiply the powers	$(a^m)^n = a^{mn}$	$(a^2)^5 = a^{10}$ $(4^3)^4 = 4^{12}$
Any non-zero number to the power zero is 1	$a^0 = 1$	$q^0 = 1$ $8^0 = 1$
Negative powers can be made positive by using the reciprocal	$a^{-n} = \dfrac{1}{a^n}$	$a^{-3} = \dfrac{1}{a^3}$ $2^{-4} = \dfrac{1}{2^4} = \dfrac{1}{16}$
Fractional powers mean roots	$a^{\frac{1}{n}} = \sqrt[n]{a}$	$a^{\frac{1}{2}}$ means the square root of a, so $25^{\frac{1}{2}} = 5$ $a^{\frac{1}{3}}$ means the cube root of a, so $64^{\frac{1}{3}} = 4$
Fractional powers may be split into finding a root, followed by finding a power*	$a^{\frac{m}{n}} = \left(a^{\frac{1}{n}}\right)^m$	$125^{\frac{2}{3}} = \left(125^{\frac{1}{3}}\right)^2 = 5^2 = 25$

*Also remember – when finding the power of a **fraction**, you find the power of both the numerator and denominator of the fraction. So $\left(\dfrac{8}{27}\right)^{\frac{1}{3}} = \dfrac{8^{\frac{1}{3}}}{27^{\frac{1}{3}}} = \dfrac{\sqrt[3]{8}}{\sqrt[3]{27}} = \dfrac{2}{3}$

Equations and identities

An equation can be solved to find an unknown quantity.

$5x + 3 = 23$ can be solved to find $x = 4$.

An **identity** is true for all values of x. $(x + 3)^2$ is identically equal to $x^2 + 6x + 9$.
You can write this as $(x + 3)^2 \equiv x^2 + 6x + 9$

Make nine cards with the letters $a, a, a, b, b, b, c, c, c$ on them. Turn all the cards face down and mix them up. Turn over two cards and multiply the letters, writing the answer algebraically, e.g. ab. Then repeat by picking three cards and multiplying the letters.

1. Simplify
   (a) $3ab - 2a^2b + 9ab + 4a^2b$
   (b) $2x - 7 + 7x - 2$
   (c) $ab + bc + ca + ac + cb + ba$

2. Simplify
   (a) $g^{12} \div g^4$
   (b) $\left(p^{15}\right)^{\frac{1}{3}}$
   (c) $2n^4a^{-3} \times 7n^{-2}a$

3. Evaluate
   (a) $8^{\frac{2}{3}}$
   (b) 4^{-2}
   (c) $\left(\dfrac{2}{3}\right)^{-3}$

Brackets

You need to be able to work with brackets:

Rule	Examples
To **multiply out** single brackets, multiply the term outside the brackets by every term inside.	$5(2a - 6) = (5 \times 2a) - (5 \times 6) = 10a - 30$ $3p(6p + 2q) = (3p \times 6p) + (3p \times 2q) = 18p^2 + 6pq$
To multiply out double brackets, multiply every term in the first bracket by every term in the second bracket.	$(2x + 3)(x - 6) = (2x \times x) + (2x \times -6) + (3 \times x) + (3 \times -6)$ $= 2x^2 - 12x + 3x - 18$ $= 2x^2 - 9x - 18$
When squaring brackets, always write out the expression in full to avoid making mistakes.	$(3x - 2)^2 = (3x - 2)(3x - 2) = 9x^2 - 6x - 6x + 4$ $= 9x^2 - 12x + 4$ $(3x - 2)^2$ is **not** equal to $9x^2 + 4$

Double brackets can also be multiplied out using a 'box method'.
For example, if you wanted to expand $(2x + 1)(3x - 2)$

×	$2x$	$+1$
$3x$	$6x^2$	$3x$
-2	$-4x$	-2

So $(2x + 1)(3x - 2) = 6x^2 + 3x - 4x - 2$
$= 6x^2 - x - 2$

Square brackets may also be multiplied out using this method.
To expand $(3 - 2p)^2$

×	3	$-2p$
3	9	$-6p$
$-2p$	$-6p$	$4p^2$

So $(3 - 2p)^2 = 9 - 6p - 6p + 4p^2$
$= 9 - 12p + 4p^2$

Factorising

Factorising is the reverse of multiplying out brackets. You have to look for the common factors in every term of the expression.

$12p + 15q = 3(4p + 5q)$ ← First look at the numbers. 12 and 15 have a highest common factor of 3. The letters are p and q, and these do not appear in both terms, so you can only 'factor out' a 3.

$6xy + 16py = 2y(3x + 8p)$ ← 6 and 16 have a highest common factor of 2. The letter y appears in both terms. So the common factor here is $2y$.

If the expression includes powers, look for the largest number and highest power that goes into each term.

$10x^2 - 5x = 5x(2x - 1)$ ← $5x$ is the largest factor of $10x^2$ and $5x$.

$6x^5 - 4x^2 = 2x^2(3x^3 - 2)$ ← 2 is the largest factor of both 6 and 4. x^2 is the highest power of x that goes into x^5 and x^2.

$18a^2b^6 - 12ab^4 = 6ab^4(3ab^2 - 2)$ ← $6ab^4$ is the largest factor of $18a^2b^6$ and $12ab^4$.

A **quadratic expression** is an expression of the form $ax^2 + bx + c$.

Factorising expressions

$x^2 + 5x - 24$ ← Look for two numbers that multiply to give −24 and add to give 5. In this case and $8 \times (-3) = -24$ and $8 + (-3) = 5$

So $x^2 + 5x - 24 = (x + 8)(x - 3)$

$x^2 + 18x + 65$ ← Look for two numbers that multiply to give 65 and add to give 18. The numbers required are 13 and 5.

So $x^2 + 18x + 65 = (x + 13)(x + 5)$

↑ Always check you have the right answer by expanding the brackets: $(x + 13)(x + 5)$ $= x^2 + 13x + 5x + 65 = x^2 + 18x + 65$

Difference of two squares

Expressions with one square subtracted from another square can be factorised. These examples all follow the pattern $a^2 - b^2 \equiv (a + b)(a - b)$, an identity known as the **difference of two squares**.

$a^2 - 9 = a^2 - 3^2 = (a + 3)(a - 3)$

$16x^2 - 25y^6 = (4x)^2 - (5y^3)^2 = (4x + 5y^3)(4x - 5y^3)$

$3a^2 - 3 = 3(a^2 - 1) = 3(a + 1)(a - 1)$

Write these six expanded expressions on separate pieces of paper and mix them up:

$x^2 + 6x + 9$	$x^2 - 9$	$x^2 - 6x - 9$
$x^2 - 6x + 9$	$x^2 + 6x - 27$	$x^2 - 9x$

Write these five factorised expressions on separate pieces of paper and mix them up:

$(x + 3)(x - 9)$ $x(x - 9)$ $(x + 3)^2$ $(x + 3)(x - 3)$ $(x - 3)^2$

Try to pair each expanded expression with the correct factorised expression. One of the expanded expressions cannot be factorised.

KEYWORDS

Multiplying out ➤ Removing brackets from an algebraic expression by multiplication.

Factorising ➤ Writing an algebraic expression as a product of factors, usually in brackets.

Difference of two squares ➤ The algebraic identity $a^2 - b^2 = (a + b)(a - b)$

1. Multiply out
   (a) $5(2 - 3x)$
   (b) $(x + 5)(x - 7)$

2. Factorise
   (a) $x^2 - x - 56$
   (b) $4p^2 - 25q^2$

3. Multiply out
   (a) $(2x + 3)(x - 1)$
   (b) $(3x + y)(3x - y)$

Using and rearranging formulae

Rearranging formulae is very similar to solving equations.

Make x the subject in the equation
$2x - y = z$

$2x = z + y$ ← Put all terms excluding x on the other side of the equation.

$x = \dfrac{z + y}{2}$ ← Divide through by 2.

Make x the subject in the equation
$\dfrac{2 - 3x}{4x + 1} = y$

If the subject appears twice in the equation, you are likely to need to factorise once all the required terms are on one side of the equation.

$2 - 3x = y(4x + 1)$ ← Clear the fraction.

$2 - 3x = 4xy + y$ ← Multiply out the brackets.

$2 = 3x + 4xy + y$ ← Collect all x terms on one side.

$2 - y = 3x + 4xy$ ← Put all terms not including x on one side.

$2 - y = x(3 + 4y)$ ← Factorise the terms involving x.

$x = \dfrac{2 - y}{3 + 4y}$ ← Divide through by $3 + 4y$.

Make x the subject in the equation
$\dfrac{5 + 12y}{x + 2y} = 8$

$5 + 12y = 8(x + 2y)$ ← Multiply through by $x + 2y$ to clear the fraction.

$5 + 12y = 8x + 16y$ ← Multiply out the brackets.

$5 - 4y = 8x$ ← Put all terms not including x on one side.

$x = \dfrac{5 - 4y}{8}$ ← Divide through by 8.

Make x the subject in the equation
$p + q = \sqrt{10x + y}$

$(p + q)^2 = 10x + y$ ← Square both sides to clear the square root sign.

$(p + q)^2 - y = 10x$ ← Put all terms not including x on one side.

$\dfrac{(p + q)^2 - y}{10} = x$ ← Divide through by 10.

Substituting numerical values in formulae

It is important to **substitute** numbers accurately into a given formula.

10

If $C = 3r^2$, find C when $r = 5$
$C = 3 \times 5^2 = 3 \times 25 = 75$ ← C is **not** $(3 \times 5)^2$. You only square the 5.

If $v = u + at$, find v when $u = 10$, $a = -2$ and $t = 8$
$v = 10 + (-2) \times 8 = 10 - 16 = -6$

If $v^2 = u^2 + 2as$, find v when $u = 5$, $a = -3$ and $s = 2$
$v^2 = 5^2 + 2 \times -3 \times 2 = 25 - 12 = 13$
So $v = \sqrt{13} = 3.61$ (2 d.p.)

If $\dfrac{1}{f} = \dfrac{1}{u} + \dfrac{1}{v}$, find v when $f = 5$ and $u = 12$

$\dfrac{1}{5} = \dfrac{1}{12} + \dfrac{1}{v}$, so $\dfrac{1}{v} = \dfrac{1}{5} - \dfrac{1}{12}$

You could rearrange this formula to make v the subject first, though it is usually easier to substitute the numbers straight in.

$\dfrac{1}{v} = \dfrac{12}{60} - \dfrac{5}{60} = \dfrac{7}{60}$

So $v = \dfrac{60}{7} = 8.57$ (2 d.p.)

Module 10   Algebraic Formulae

Translating procedures into expressions or formulae

You may be asked to derive a formula from some given information.

A motorist wishes to rent a car. The rental cost is £35 per day, plus a standing charge of £60. Write down an expression for the total cost, £C, in terms of the number of days, d. For how many days can the motorist rent the car if he has £400 to spend?

The total cost is $C = 60 + 35d$

If $C = 400$, then you need to solve the equation $400 = 60 + 35d$

So $340 = 35d$ and $d = \dfrac{340}{35} = 9.71$

The motorist can rent the car for a maximum of 9 days.

The angles in a quadrilateral, in degrees, are $6y + 16$, $24 + y$, $106 - y$ and 130. Form an equation and use it to find the value of y.

The interior angles of a quadrilateral add up to $360°$, so $6y + 16 + 24 + y + 106 - y + 130 = 360$

Therefore $6y + 276 = 360$

So $6y = 84$ and $y = \dfrac{84}{6} = 14°$

S is the total sum of the interior angles in a regular polygon. If the polygon has n sides, find an expression for S in terms of n.

If the polygon has n sides, then it can be split up into $n - 2$ triangles.

For example, a regular six-sided hexagon can be split into four triangles.

The interior angles of each triangle add up to $180°$, therefore $S = 180(n - 2)$

1. Make p the subject in each of the following formulae.

    (a) $3p + a = b$
    (b) $q = \dfrac{3p + 2}{2p + 3}$

2. If $a = -10$, $b = 20$ and $c = 4$, find the exact values for p when

    (a) $p = a^2 - c^2$
    (b) $p = \dfrac{a + c}{b}$

3. A triangle has interior angles of size $3x$, $x - 2$ and $2x - 10$.
    (a) Write down an equation in x.
    (b) Solve the equation to find x.
    (c) Find the values of the three angles.

The area of a trapezium is given by $A = \dfrac{(a + b)h}{2}$

Write each letter and symbol in this equation on separate pieces of card. You will also need a card with the minus symbol on it. Rearrange the letters and symbols to make a the subject of the equation. Then do the same to make b the subject and finally to make h the subject.

Solving linear equations

To solve any **linear equation**, you rearrange it to make x the subject.

> Remember to do the same operation to both sides of the equation.

Solve $3x + 4 = 25$

$$3x = 21 \quad \longleftarrow \text{Subtract 4 from both sides.}$$

$$x = 7 \quad \longleftarrow \text{Divide both sides by 3.}$$

Solve $12x - 9 = 4x + 11$

$$8x - 9 = 11 \quad \longleftarrow \text{Subtract } 4x \text{ from both sides.}$$

$$8x = 20 \quad \longleftarrow \text{Add 9 to both sides.}$$

$$x = \frac{20}{8} = \frac{5}{2} \quad \longleftarrow \text{Divide both sides by 8.}$$

Solve $5(x - 1) + 2(3x + 4) = 36$

$$5x - 5 + 6x + 8 = 36 \quad \longleftarrow \text{Multiply out the brackets.}$$

$$11x + 3 = 36 \quad \longleftarrow \text{Collect 'like terms'.}$$

$$11x = 33 \quad \longleftarrow \text{Subtract 3 from both sides.}$$

$$x = \frac{33}{11} \quad \longleftarrow \text{Divide both sides by 11.}$$

$$x = 3$$

KEYWORDS

Linear equation ➤ An equation where each term is a multiple of one variable or a constant number.

Quadratic equation ➤ An equation where each term is a multiple of x^2, a multiple of x or a constant number.

Simultaneous equations ➤ A pair of equations in two unknowns.

Elimination ➤ A method of solving simultaneous equations by eliminating either x or y.

Choose a positive whole number b.

Write down the quadratic equation $x^2 - 2bx + b^2 = 0$ using your value of b.

Try to solve your equation. What do you notice?

Now try this again with a different value for b. Does the same thing happen again? Can you see why?

Solving quadratic equations

Quadratic equations are usually written in the form $ax^2 + bx + c = 0$, where a, b and c are numbers.

Solving by factorising $\longleftarrow$

> Factorising uses the idea that if two expressions multiplied together gives 0, then one of the expressions must be equal to 0.

Solve $x^2 + 11x + 18 = 0$

$(x + 9)(x + 2) = 0 \quad \longleftarrow$ Factorise the left-hand side.

So $x + 9 = 0$ or $x + 2 = 0$

Therefore $x = -9$ or $x = -2$

Solve $x^2 - 12x + 35 = 0$

$(x - 5)(x - 7) = 0$

So $x - 5 = 0$ or $x - 7 = 0$

Therefore $x = 5$ or $x = 7$

Solve $x^2 + 7x - 18 = 0$

$(x + 9)(x - 2) = 0$

So $x + 9 = 0$ or $x - 2 = 0$

Therefore $x = -9$ or $x = 2$

Solve $x^2 - 64 = 0 \quad \longleftarrow$

> Watch out for the 'difference of two squares'.

$(x + 8)(x - 8) = 0 \quad \longleftarrow$ Factorise.

So $x + 8 = 0$ or $x - 8 = 0$

Therefore $x = -8$ or $x = 8$

Module 11 Algebraic Equations

Algebraic Equations

Module 11

Simultaneous linear equations

You can solve **simultaneous equations** by **elimination**.

Solve the simultaneous equations
$$3x + 5y = 23$$
$$3x + 2y = 11$$

The coefficients of x and y are the same (equal to 3) so **subtract** both equations to eliminate x.

$3y = 12$ ← Now divide both sides by 3.

$y = 4$ ← Now substitute $y = 4$ back into either of the original equations. If you choose the second equation: $3x + 8 = 11$ so $3x = 3$ and $x = 1$

The solution is therefore $x = 1$, $y = 4$

To check these values are correct, you can substitute them into either of the initial equations:

$3 \times 1 + 5 \times 4 = 23$ $3 \times 1 + 2 \times 4 = 11$

Solve the simultaneous equations

$2x - 5y = 23$

$x + y = 1$ ← The coefficients of x or those of y must be the same to **eliminate** them. Here neither are the same but the 2nd equation can be multiplied by 2.

$2x - 5y = 23$

$2x + 2y = 2$ ← Now the coefficients of x are both 2, so **subtract** to eliminate x.

$-7y = 21$, so $y = -3$

$x + y = 1$ ← Substitute $y = -3$ back into either of the original equations.

$x - 3 = 1$, so $x = 4$

So the solutions are $x = 4$, $y = -3$

To check these are correct:

$2 \times 4 - 5 \times (-3) = 23$ $4 + (-3) = 1$

Callie regularly visits the sweet shop. One week she bought five chocolate bars and three bags of fruit drops, costing £5.95. The next week she bought two chocolate bars and one bag of fruit drops, costing £2.25. Find the cost of one chocolate bar and one bag of fruit drops.

Let c = the cost of one chocolate bar

Let d = the cost of one bag of fruit drops

Then $5c + 3d = 595$

And $2c + d = 225$ ← Set up two equations using the information given in the question.

Rewrite as:

$6c + 3d = 675$ ← Multiplying the second equation by 3.

And $5c + 3d = 595$ ← Leave the first equation as it is. You now have $3d$ in each equation.

So $c = 80$ ← Subtracting these two equations gives the cost of one chocolate bar (80p).

Finally, $2 \times 80 + d = 225$, or $160 + d = 225$

So $d = 65$ ← 65p is the cost of one bag of fruit drops.

Using graphs to solve quadratic equations

Graphs can be used to solve equations by looking at their points of intersections with the x-axis or with each other.

This graph shows the equation
$y = x^2 + 5x + 3$
Use it to solve the equation $x^2 + 5x + 3 = 0$

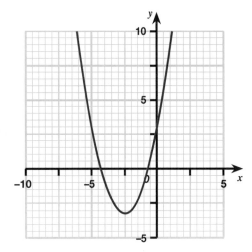

$x^2 + 5x + 3 = 0$ is where the curve crosses the x-axis, so the solutions are (approx.) $x = -4.3$ and $x = -0.8$

By drawing a straight line on the same grid you can solve $x^2 + 4x - 2 = 0$

Start with the equation **you are trying to solve**, and add or subtract x^2 terms, x terms and numbers to obtain the equation **you are given**.

Adding $x + 5$ to both sides of $x^2 + 4x - 2 = 0$ gives $x^2 + 5x + 3 = x + 5$ ←

You already have the graph of $y = x^2 + 5x + 3$, so plot $y = x + 5$ and find the x-coordinates of the point(s) of intersection. You will find the solutions are (approx.) $x = -4.5$ and $x = 0.5$

1. Solve these equations.
   (a) $7(x - 2) = 35$
   (b) $4 - 2x = 5 - 5x$

2. Solve the equation $x^2 - 11x + 10 = 0$

3. Solve the simultaneous equations
   $$4x - y = 13$$
   $$3x + y = 1$$

4. Solve the equation $\dfrac{x + 1}{2} + \dfrac{x - 4}{3} = \dfrac{10}{3}$

Inequality symbols

The **inequality** symbols are:

< means less than	⩽ means less than or equal to
> means greater than	⩾ means greater than or equal to

Solving linear inequalities in one variable

Linear inequalities are solved in the same way as linear equations, with one main exception: when multiplying or dividing by a negative number, you change the direction of the inequality symbol.

Solve the inequality $5x + 4 \geqslant 2x - 20$

$3x + 4 \geqslant -20$ ← Subtract $2x$ from both sides.

$3x \geqslant -24$ ← Subtract 4 from both sides.

$x \geqslant -8$ ← Divide by 3.

Solve the inequality $x + 33 > 4x + 24$

$33 > 3x + 24$ ← Subtract x from both sides.

$9 > 3x$ ← Subtract 24 from both sides.

$3 > x$ ← Divide both sides by 3.

$x < 3$ ← Rewrite the inequality starting with x (3 is greater than x means that x is less than 3).

Solve the inequality $12 - 5x > 7$

$-5x > -5$ ← Subtract 12 from both sides.

$x < 1$ ← Both sides are divided by a negative number (–5) so the direction of the inequality is changed.

Each of these solutions may be represented on a number line.

$x \geqslant -8$ is represented by a 'filled-in' circle (since –8 is included) and an arrow to the right.

$x < 3$ is represented by a 'hollow' circle (since 3 is excluded) and an arrow to the left.

$x < 1$ is represented by a 'hollow' circle and an arrow to the left.

Module 12 — Algebraic Inequalities

12

Module 12

Inequalities involving fractions

If the inequality involves fractions, you should 'multiply through' to remove the fractions.

Solve the inequality $\dfrac{5x - 9}{3} > 2$

$5x - 9 > 6$ ← Multiply both sides by 3.

$5x > 15$ ← Add 9 to both sides.

$x > 3$ ← Divide both sides by 5.

Two inequalities

If there are two inequalities, then divide the inequality into two parts and solve each part separately.

Solve $5 < 4x - 3 \leqslant 21$

Split this into $5 < 4x - 3$ and $4x - 3 \leqslant 21$

$5 < 4x - 3$	$4x - 3 \leqslant 21$
$8 < 4x$	$4x \leqslant 24$
$2 < x$	$x \leqslant 6$

So the solution can be written as $2 < x \leqslant 6$

The integer values that satisfy this inequality are $x = 3$, $x = 4$, $x = 5$ and $x = 6$. On a number line:

Solve $1 < \dfrac{3x - 1}{2} < 16$

Split this into $1 < \dfrac{3x - 1}{2}$ and $\dfrac{3x - 1}{2} < 16$

$2 < 3x - 1$	$3x - 1 < 32$
$3 < 3x$	$3x < 33$
$1 < x$	$x < 11$

So the solution is $1 < x < 11$

KEYWORDS

Inequality ➤ A relationship when one quantity is greater or less than another.

Linear inequality ➤ An inequality involving only x terms and numbers.

Chalk a number line from –5 to 5 on the ground. Practise showing these solutions to inequalities using filled-in circles, hollow circles and arrows:

$x \geqslant 1$ $x < 2$ $x > -4$ $x \leqslant 3$

---

1. Solve the inequalities:
   (a) $4x - 9 < x + 15$
   (b) $8 - 9x \geqslant 33 + x$

2. Write down the inequalities shown by these number lines:

   (a)

   (b)

3. Solve the inequality $2(x - 6) < 5(4 - 2x)$ and show your solution on a number line.

Term-to-term and position-to-term sequences

A term-to-term **sequence** means you can find a rule for each **term** based on the previous term(s) in the sequence.

$$U_{n+1} = U_n + 4, \ U_1 = 3 \leftarrow$$

> This means the next term in the sequence is found by adding 4 to the previous term, and the first term is 3.

> U_n just means 'the nth term in the sequence'.

The sequence is 3, 7, 11, 15, 19, 23, …

In a position-to-term sequence, you can find a rule for each term based on its position in the sequence.

$$U_n = 8n - 2 \leftarrow$$

> Remember, U_n means 'the nth term in the sequence'.

> To find the first term, you substitute $n = 1$. To find the second term, you substitute $n = 2$, and so on.

The sequence is 6, 14, 22, 30, 38, …

Consider the term-to-term sequence $U_{n+1} = 3U_n$ with $U_1 = 2$ ←

> In this sequence, the first term is 2 and you multiply by 3 to go from one term to the next.

First term in the sequence $\longrightarrow$ $U_1 = 2$
Second term in the sequence $\longrightarrow$ $U_2 = 3U_1 = 3 \times 2 = 6$
Third term in the sequence $\longrightarrow$ $U_3 = 3U_2 = 3 \times 6 = 18$
Fourth term in the sequence $\longrightarrow$ $U_4 = 3U_3 = 3 \times 18 = 54$

The sequence is 2, 6, 18, 54, 162, … ←

> The next term will be $162 \times 3 = 486$

This sequence may also be expressed using a position-to-term formula.
The formula is $U_n = 2 \times 3^{n-1}$. In other words, the nth term in the sequence is $2 \times 3^{n-1}$.

$$U_1 = 2 \times 3^{1-1} = 2 \qquad U_2 = 2 \times 3^{2-1} = 6 \qquad U_3 = 2 \times 3^{3-1} = 18 \qquad U_4 = 2 \times 3^{4-1} = 54$$

Standard sequences

Square numbers 1, 4, 9, 16, 25, …	$U_n = n^2$ This sequence is produced by squaring the numbers 1, 2, 3, 4, 5, … etc.	
Cube numbers 1, 8, 27, 64, 125, …	$U_n = n^3$ This sequence is produced by cubing the numbers 1, 2, 3, 4, 5, … etc.	
Triangular numbers 1, 3, 6, 10, 15, 21, …	$U_n = \dfrac{n(n+1)}{2}$ This sequence is generated from a pattern of dots that form a triangle.	
Fibonacci sequence 1, 1, 2, 3, 5, 8, 13, 21, …	$U_{n+2} = U_{n+1} + U_n$ and $U_1 = U_2 = 1$ The next number is found by adding the two previous numbers. So the next number in the sequence would be $13 + 21 = 34$.	There are other 'types' of Fibonacci sequence. One is the Lucas series: 2, 1, 3, 4, 7, 11, 18, … The term-to-term formula is the same as the original Fibonacci sequence, i.e. $U_{n+2} = U_{n+1} + U_n$, though in this case $U_1 = 2$ and $U_2 = 1$

The Fibonacci sequence is also a type of **recursive sequence** as finding the next term requires you to know previous terms.

Arithmetic sequences

An **arithmetic sequence** is a sequence of numbers having a common first difference.

Sequence   4 7 10 13 16 ← Here there is a common first difference of 3.

For any arithmetic sequence, the position-to-term formula is given by $U_n = dn + (a - d)$, where a is the first term and d is the common difference.

So here $U_n = 3n + (4 - 3)$, i.e. $U_n = 3n + 1$ ← The next number in the sequence will therefore be $U_6 = 3 \times 6 + 1 = 19$

Geometric sequences

In a **geometric sequence** you multiply by a constant number (common ratio) r to go from one term to the next.

3   9   27   81   243
$\times 3$ $\times 3$ $\times 3$ $\times 3$

Each number is multiplied by 3 each time, so the common ratio $r = 3$

The term-to-term formula is $U_{n+1} = 3U_n$ with $U_1 = 3$

The position-to-term formula is $U_n = 3^n$

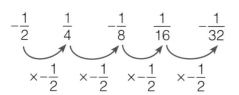

$-\dfrac{1}{2}$ $\dfrac{1}{4}$ $-\dfrac{1}{8}$ $\dfrac{1}{16}$ $-\dfrac{1}{32}$
$\times -\dfrac{1}{2}$ $\times -\dfrac{1}{2}$ $\times -\dfrac{1}{2}$ $\times -\dfrac{1}{2}$

The common ratio $r = -\dfrac{1}{2}$

The term-to-term formula is $U_{n+1} = -\dfrac{U_n}{2}$ with $U_1 = -\dfrac{1}{2}$

The position-to-term formula is $U_n = \left(-\dfrac{1}{2}\right)^n$

One problem that uses sequences is called the 'handshake problem'.

Draw three people in a triangle.

If every person shakes hand with each other, how many handshakes will there?

Now draw four people in a square. Again, how many handshakes will there be?

If n is the number of people, it can be shown that the position-to-term formula for the number of handshakes is $U_n = \dfrac{n^2}{2} - \dfrac{n}{2}$

How many handshakes would take place if there were six people? Check by drawing a diagram **and** using the formula.

13

1. Find the first three terms in the sequence given by $U_n = \dfrac{n^3 - 1}{2}$

2. The sequence 4, 13, 22, 31, 40, … forms an arithmetic sequence.
   (a) Find an expression for U_n, the position-to-term formula.
   (b) Now find an exact value for U_{100}, the 100th term in the sequence.
   (c) Is 779 a number in this sequence? Explain your answer.

KEYWORDS

Sequence ➤ A series of numbers following a mathematical pattern.

Term ➤ A number in a sequence.

Arithmetic sequence ➤ A sequence with a common first difference between consecutive terms.

Geometric sequence ➤ A sequence with a common ratio.

Coordinates

Coordinates are used to describe any point in two-dimensional space. They are written using brackets (x, y). The x-coordinate tells you how far to the **right** the coordinate is, and the y-coordinate tells you how far **up**.

The x-axis and y-axis split the space into four quadrants. Here are examples of coordinates in each quadrant.

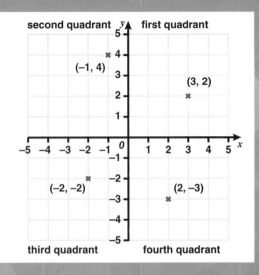

Graphs of straight lines

To plot a straight-line graph, you should first draw up a table of values.

Plot the graph of $y = -2x + 4$

x	0	1	2	3
y	4	2	0	-2

Plot the points and draw the line.

Take some simple values for x, perhaps 0, 1, 2 and 3, and calculate y for each value. For example, when $x = 3$, $y = -2 \times 3 + 4 = -2$

$y = mx + c$

The equation of any straight line can be written as $y = mx + c$ where m is the **gradient** and c is the point of intercept with the y-axis.

In the example above, the gradient m is -2 and the y-intercept, c, is 4. So the equation is $y = -2x + 4$

You need to be able to calculate both the gradient and the y-intercept from a given graph.

Find the equation of this straight line.

To find the gradient, take any two points on the line. Here we have chosen $(0, 3)$ and $(4, 5)$.

$$m = \frac{\text{change in } y}{\text{change in } x} = \frac{2}{4} = \frac{1}{2}$$

The graph crosses the y-axis at $(0, 3)$ so $c = 3$

Therefore, the equation of the line is $y = \frac{1}{2}x + 3$

Gradient ➤ The gradient, or slope, of a straight line shows how steep it is.

The gradient is equal to the $\frac{\text{change in } y}{\text{change in } x}$

Coordinates ➤ A pair of numbers (in brackets) used to determine a point in a plane.

Parallel ➤ Two lines are parallel if they have the same gradient. Parallel lines can never meet.

Finding the equation of a line through two given points

Here is a line going through the points (−2, 5) and (4, 1).

The gradient

$$m = \frac{\text{change in } y}{\text{change in } x} = \frac{-4}{6} = -\frac{2}{3}$$

Now the equation of the line is $y = mx + c$,

or $y = -\dfrac{2}{3}x + c$

Notice from (−2, 5) to (4, 1), the y value decreases, so the change in y is negative. The gradient is negative since the line slopes downwards.

Substituting $x = 4$, $y = 1$ gives $1 = -\dfrac{8}{3} + c$,

so $c = \dfrac{11}{3}$

This can be written as $3y = −2x + 11$

The equation of the line is therefore $y = -\dfrac{2}{3}x + \dfrac{11}{3}$

Chalk two sets of x and y axes on the ground. On one set of axes, chalk a straight line going diagonally 'uphill'. On the second set of axes, chalk a straight line going diagonally 'downhill'. Pace out the changes in x and y to work out the rough gradient of each diagonal line.

Finding the equation of a line through one point with a given gradient

Find the equation of the line with gradient 3, going through (2, 4).

The equation of the line is $y = mx + c$, or $y = 3x + c$.

$4 = 3 \times 2 + c$ ← Now substitute the **coordinates** of the point to find c, i.e. use $x = 2$ and $y = 4$

$4 = 6 + c$

So $c = -2$ and the equation of the line is $y = 3x - 2$

Parallel lines

Two lines are **parallel** if they have the same gradient. For example, $y = 2x + 1$, $y = 2x$ and $y = 2x - 3$ are all parallel.

A line L is parallel to the line $y = 2x + 4$ and passes through the point (2, 7). Find the equation of L.

Since both lines are parallel, they both have the same gradient, and so L has gradient $m = 2$

So L has equation $y = 2x + c$

Substituting $x = 2$ and $y = 7$ gives $7 = 2 \times 2 + c$, or $7 = 4 + c$

So $c = 3$ and L has equation $y = 2x + 3$

1. A line has gradient 3 and goes through the point (0, −2).
   Write down the equation of the line.
2. Three lines are given by $4y = 8 - x$, $y = 2x + 16$ and $4y = 8x - 1$.
   Which two lines are parallel?
3. A line has gradient 4 and goes through the point (8, 0). Find the equation of the line.
4. Find the equation of the line joining points (−2, −6) to (6, 12).

Roots and intercepts

A quadratic function has the equation
$y = ax^2 + bx + c$

If $a > 0$, the graph will look like:

If $a < 0$, the graph will look like:

A quadratic function may also cross the x-axis twice (e.g. $y = x^2 - 6x + 5$), once (e.g. $y = x^2 - 4x + 4$) or not at all (e.g. $y = x^2 - 5x + 8$). However, it will always cross the y-axis at some point once.

Roots and **intercepts** of a quadratic function may be found graphically or algebraically.

This is the graph of
$y = x^2 - 2x - 3$

The graph crosses the x-axis twice, at $x = -1$ and $x = 3$. These are the roots of the equation $x^2 - 2x - 3 = 0$.
The intercept with the y-axis occurs at (0, –3).

Consider the function $y = x^2 - 11x + 18$
To find the roots, factorise $x^2 - 11x + 18 = 0$
By factorising, you obtain $(x - 9)(x - 2) = 0$
$x - 9 = 0$ or $x - 2 = 0$
So the roots are $x = 9$ and $x = 2$

The curve crosses the y-axis when $x = 0$
So substituting $x = 0$ in the original equation: $y = 0^2 - 11 \times 0 + 18 = 18$.

Therefore, the graph will intercept the y-axis at (0, 18).

Turning points

Every quadratic equation has a **turning point** at a minimum (if $a > 0$) or maximum point (if $a < 0$).

Finding a turning point graphically

The turning point on the curve
$y = x^2 - 2x - 3$
is a minimum point and occurs at (1, –4).

Turning point

The symmetrical property of a quadratic

Every quadratic graph $y = ax^2 + bx + c$ has a line of symmetry occurring at $x = -\dfrac{b}{2a}$

The roots also occur at an equal distance either side of the line $x = -\dfrac{b}{2a}$ ← It is also true that this is also the x-coordinate of the turning point on the curve.

Finding a line of symmetry

Find the equation of the line of symmetry of the curve
$y = 3x^2 - 8x + 10$ ← $a = 3$ and $b = -8$

So the line of symmetry is $x = -\dfrac{b}{2a} = -\left(\dfrac{-8}{6}\right) = \dfrac{4}{3}$

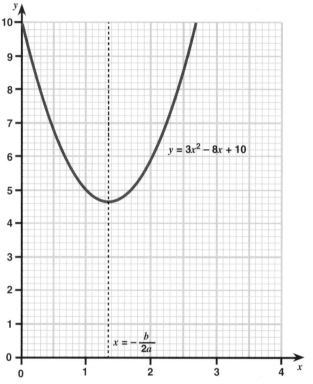

$y = 3x^2 - 8x + 10$

$x = -\dfrac{b}{2a}$

Draw a set of x-y axes on an A3 sheet of paper. Pick two specific points on the x-axis and one point on the y-axis. Draw a quadratic curve going through these points. Try to find the equation of the curve you have drawn.

1. Consider the curve $y = x^2 - 3x - 40$
   (a) Find the coordinates of the points where the curve intersects the x-axis.
   (b) State the coordinates where the curve crosses the y-axis.
   (c) Find the equation of the line of symmetry of the curve.
2. Consider the curve $y = x^2 + 10x - 40$
   (a) Find the equation of the line of symmetry of the curve.
   (b) Now find the coordinates of the turning point on the curve.

Functions

A **function** maps one number to another number.

Consider the function 'add 3'.

Input x		Output $f(x)$
1	maps to	4
2	maps to	5
3	maps to	6
4	maps to	7

It is represented graphically by plotting $y = x + 3$

This can be written as $f(x) = x + 3$

Consider the function 'square and subtract 2'.

Input x		Output $f(x)$
0	→	–2
1	→	–1
2	→	2
3	→	7

This can be written as $f(x) = x^2 - 2$
i.e. $f(0) = -2$, $f(1) = -1$, etc.

As well as **linear functions** $f(x) = ax + b$ and **quadratic functions** $f(x) = ax^2 + bx + c$, there are other types of function you need to know.

Cubic functions

Cubic functions have the form $y = ax^3 + bx^2 + cx + d$

The simplest cubic function is $y = x^3$

When $a > 0$, cubic functions generally have this shape.

$y = x^3 + 2x^2 - 5x - 4$

For $a < 0$, the graph would look like a reflection of this.

On A4 paper, draw an 'Input' column from 0 to 5, and a blank 'Output' column.

Try to find a function that has fewer than six different outputs for these inputs. Can you find more than one such function?

Reciprocal functions

Reciprocal functions have the form $y = \dfrac{k}{x}$ where k is a constant number. There are two types of curve, depending if k is positive or negative.

$y = \dfrac{2}{x}$

$y = \dfrac{-3}{x}$

Each section of the graph approaches both axes and they are symmetrical about the line $y = x$

Each section of the graph again approaches both axes but they are in opposite quadrants to when $k > 0$. These graphs are symmetrical about $y = -x$

KEYWORDS

Function ➤ A type of mapping sending a number (input) to another number (output).

Linear function ➤ A mapping of the form $f(x) = ax + b$

Quadratic function ➤ A mapping of the form $f(x) = ax^2 + bx + c$

Cubic function ➤ A mapping of the form $f(x) = ax^3 + bx^2 + cx + d$

Reciprocal function ➤ A mapping of the form $f(x) = \dfrac{k}{x}$

---

1. For the function $f(x) = 5 - x$, write down the outputs for each of the following inputs:

Input x		Output $f(x)$
−1	⟶	
0	⟶	
1	⟶	
2	⟶	

2. Find the function given by the following mapping:

Input x		Output $f(x)$
1	⟶	7
2	⟶	9
3	⟶	11
4	⟶	13

3. Match the correct graph to each function:

$$f(x) = \frac{2}{x} \qquad f(x) = \frac{1}{x} \qquad f(x) = \frac{-2}{x}$$

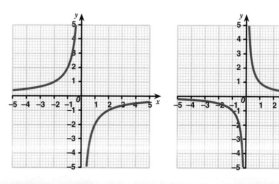

Practical problems involving graphs

This graph shows how the value of a new car changes over time:

Find the **rate of depreciation** of the car.

In six years, the car's value reduces from £12 000 to £3000, a difference of £9000.

The rate of depreciation is therefore $\frac{9000}{6}$ = £1500 per year.

The opposite of a rate of depreciation is a **rate of appreciation**.

KEYWORDS

Rate of appreciation
➤ The rate an object's value increases.

Rate of depreciation
➤ The rate an object's value decreases.

Distance–time graph
➤ A graph that shows how distance varies with time.

Distance–time and speed–time graphs

In a **distance–time graph**, the gradient represents the **speed** at a given time.

The graph opposite shows Max travelling to his friend's house.

(a) Find the speed at which Max walks to his friend's house.

The gradient of the first line is $\frac{1.5}{0.5}$ = 3km/h

(b) Find the speed at which he returns.

The gradient of the final line is $\frac{1.5}{2}$ = 0.75km/h

In a **speed–time graph**, the gradient represents the **acceleration** at a given time.

The area under a speed–time graph represents the distance the object has travelled.

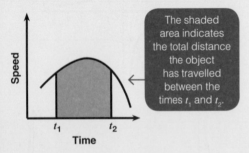

The shaded area indicates the total distance the object has travelled between the times t_1 and t_2.

The graph above right shows the speed of an object at time t.

(a) Find the acceleration of the object.

The gradient of the line is $\frac{2}{6} = \frac{1}{3}$

So the acceleration is $\frac{1}{3}$m/s²

(b) Find the total distance travelled by the object.

The area under the graph is that of a trapezium.

The area is $\frac{1}{2} \times (1 + 3) \times 6$ = 12

So the total distance travelled is 12m.

Module 17 Problems and Graphs (side tab)

An object travels in a straight line from rest such that its speed s at time t is given by $s = t \times 2^{-t}$ for $t \geqslant 0$.

The graph of s against t is shown.

(a) Find the speed of the object after 4 seconds.

From the graph, you can see that when $t = 4$, $s = 1\,\text{m/s}$.

(b) Find the time(s) when the speed of the object is $2\,\text{m/s}$.

By drawing a straight line across from $s = 2$, you can see that this intersects the curve in two places, namely when $t = 0.6\text{s}$ and $t = 2\text{s}$

1. The graphs A, B, C, D and E show how the populations have changed in five different countries. Match each country to its description.
   1 – The population increased steadily over time.
   2 – The population remained steady and did not increase or decrease over time.
   3 – The population decreased at a quick rate after decreasing quite slowly.
   4 – The population increased slowly at first but then increased at a quicker rate.
   5 – The population decreased at a constant rate.

2. The graph opposite shows the speed of a cyclist over 15 seconds.
   (a) For how long is the cyclist travelling at a constant speed?
   (b) Calculate the deceleration of the cyclist.
   (c) Calculate the total distance travelled by the cyclist.

Imagine a skydiver jumping out of an aeroplane. After falling halfway to the ground, he opens his parachute and continues to fall, before safely reaching the ground. On a large sheet of paper, draw a set of axes, marking the x-axis as time and the y-axis as speed. Try to draw the speed–time graph for the skydiver, marking the point where the skydiver opens his parachute.

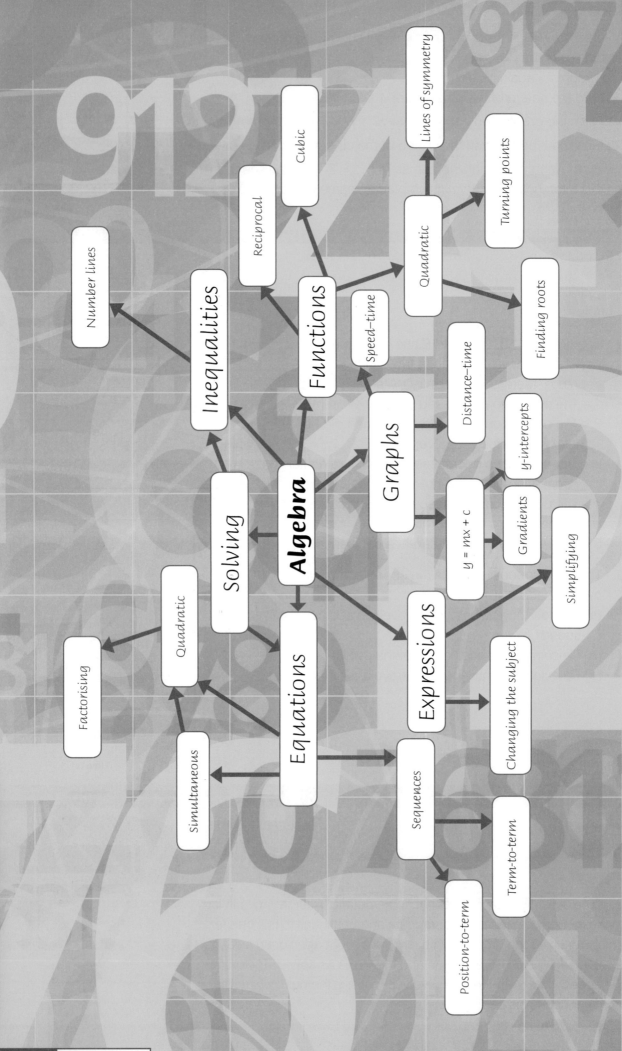

1. Solve the following equations.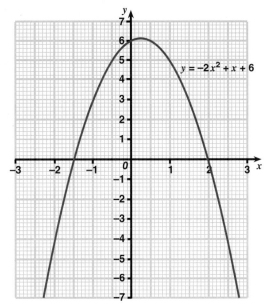
    (a) $3(x - 2) - 4(x - 1) = 0$ **[2]**
    (b) $\dfrac{x + 8}{3} = \dfrac{2x - 9}{5}$ **[3]**

2. Which of the following lines are parallel? **[2]**

    A: | $3y = x - 6$ | **B:** | $4x + 2y = 8$ |

    C: | $x = 3y - 12$ | **D:** | $2y - x + 2 = 0$ |

3. Given the formula $S = 6r^2h$, work out the value of S when $r = 2$ and $h = 0.5$ **[2]**

4. Factorise fully $18a^2 - 6ab$ **[2]**

5. The following graph shows a quadratic curve $y = f(x)$

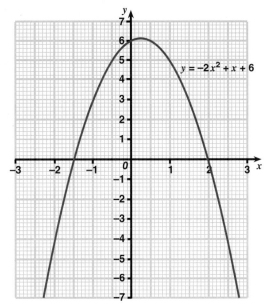

$y = -2x^2 + x + 6$

    From the information in the graph, write down:
    (a) The roots of $f(x) = 0$ **[2]**
    (b) The coordinates of the y-intercept. **[1]**
    (c) The equation of the line of symmetry. **[1]**

6. Solve the following equations by factorisation:
    (a) $x^2 + 16x + 63 = 0$ **[3]**
    (b) $x^2 + 7x - 30 = 0$ **[3]**

7. Find the next term in the following sequence.
    5   21   47   83   129 **[2]**

8. If $y = \dfrac{3x + 1}{x - 2}$, make x the subject. **[3]**

9. Solve the simultaneous equations $2x + 3y = 1$
                                  $3x - 2y = -18$ **[4]**

10. **(a)** Sketch the curve of $y = \dfrac{4}{x}$ **[2]**
    (b) What straight line should you draw on the same axes in order to solve the equation $x^2 + x = 4$? **[3]**

Algebra

Metric and imperial units

In the UK we still use a mix of different units and you need to know some standard conversions between the two systems.

Length	2.5cm ≈ 1 inch	8km ≈ 5 miles
Volume	1 litre ≈ $1\frac{3}{4}$ pts	4.5 litres ≈ 1 gallon
Mass	1kg ≈ 2.2lb	28g ≈ 1 ounce

Time

60s = 1 minute
60 mins = 1 hour
24h = 1 day
365 days = 1 year

> Be very careful with time. Your calculator may give an answer of 2.25 hours. This is **not** 2h 25min but $2\frac{1}{4}$ h which is 2h 15min. If you have to enter 3h 30min into your calculator, this is 3.5h **not** 3.30h.

The metric system

Metric measures are based on units of 10.

milli... means $\frac{1}{1000}$	*centi...* means $\frac{1}{100}$	*kilo...* means 1000

Mass: 1000g = 1kg   and   1000kg = 1 tonne
Length: 1000mm = 100cm = 1m   and   1000m = 1km
Capacity: 1000ml = 1 litre   and   1000 litres = $1m^3$

Currency conversions

You must always use your common sense. Conversions are always given as a ratio, e.g. £1 : $1.60

Imagine the bank taking away your £1 coin and giving you $1.60 instead. You have more dollars than you had pounds (although they are worth the same).

Convert £450 to $ 450 × 1.6 = $720 ← More dollars than pounds

Convert $620 to £   620 ÷ 1.6 = £387.50 ← More dollars than pounds

Compound units

You need to know about speed, density, pressure and rates of pay.

Speed = $\frac{distance}{time}$ so the units will always be 'distance' per 'time'.

metres per second	centimetres per second	km per hour	miles per hour	feet per second
m/s or ms⁻¹	cm/s or cms⁻¹	km/h or kmh⁻¹	mph	ft/s or fts⁻¹

Density = $\frac{mass}{volume}$ so the units will always be 'mass' per 'volume', e.g. kg/m^3 (or kgm^{-3}) and g/cm^3 (or gcm^{-3}).

Pressure = $\frac{force}{area}$ (units include Newtons/m²)

Rates of pay are given for a unit of time so £18/h or £500/week or £4400/month or £33 000/annum.

Converting between **compound units** should always be done in steps.

Change 80km/h into m/s.		
	80km	in 1 hour
is	80 000m	in 1 hour
is	80 000m	in 60min
is	1333.333...m	in 1min
is	22.22...m	in 1s
So 80km/h is 22.2m/s (3 s.f.)		

Module 18   Converting Measurements

Conversions for area and volume

A diagram always helps when converting between different units for area and volume.

Area

Filling a 1m² with cm²
➤ 100 rows of 100
➤ 10 000cm² (10⁴ cm²) in 1m²

Filling a 1cm² with mm²
➤ 10 rows of 10
➤ 100mm² in 1cm²

Filling a 1m² with mm²
➤ 1000 rows of 1000
➤ 1 000 000mm² (10⁶ mm²) in 1m²

Volume

Imagine filling a box
1m × 1m × 1m with tiny cubes
each 1cm × 1cm × 1cm.
There would be 100 rows of
100 on the bottom layer and
100 layers.
There are 1 000 000cm³ in 1m³.

Imagine filling a box
1cm × 1cm × 1cm with tiny
cubes each
1mm × 1mm × 1mm.
There would be 10 rows of 10 on
the bottom layer and 10 layers.
There are 1000mm³ in 1cm³.

Imagine filling a box
1m³ with mm³.
There would be
1000 rows of 1000 and
1000 layers.
There are 1 000 000 000mm³
(10⁹) in 1m³.

KEYWORDS

Compound units ➤ A measurement
unit using more than one quantity,
often using 'per' as in speed, e.g.
km/h (kilometres per hour).

Measure some water into a measuring
jug. Weigh the jug of water and then
weigh the jug empty. Work out the
weight of the water and calculate its
density in either g/cm³ or kg/m³.

1. Convert 64km/h to m/s.
2. Amil sees some jeans for sale in France for
   €80. If they cost £48 in the UK, where should
   he buy them? (£1 = €1.25)
3. Convert 8400mm² to cm².
4. Convert 2.5m³ to cm³.

Scale factors

You will meet scale factors in **scale drawings**, **similar triangles** and in **enlargements**.

A scale diagram is an accurate drawing, the scale tells you how the lengths in the diagram relate to real life. They are usually given as a ratio in the form 1: n

	Typical scale	…represents…
An atlas	1:10 000 000	1cm to 100km
A road map	1:250 000	1cm to 2.5km
An Ordnance Survey Explorer map	1:25 000	1cm to 250m
An architect's plan	1:100	1cm to 1m
A modeller's plan	1:24	1cm to 24cm

Scale factors and diagrams

If you have to calculate a distance from a map or plan:
➤ Measure the distance accurately with a ruler
➤ Write down the scale given
➤ Calculate the scaled-up 'real' size.

If you have to draw a map or plan:
➤ Decide on a suitable scale
➤ Write down the 'real' distances
➤ Calculate the scaled-down lengths
➤ Draw the plan accurately.

Scale 1 : 20 000

The distance between the Round Pond and Lancaster Gate station is 4cm.

In real life this is 800m.

> **Beware!**
>
> The angles are always the same in both the plan and real life.
>
> The areas on a scale drawing will be reduced by [scale factor]^2 – see Module 18.

KEYWORDS

Scale drawing ➤ A drawing used to represent a larger (or smaller) shape.

Similar triangles ➤ Triangles with corresponding angles equal and corresponding sides in the same ratio.

Enlargement ➤ A transformation that changes the size of an object using a scale factor and (usually) a centre of enlargement.

Bearings

Use bearings to set an absolute direction, measured from compass North. You always start at a point with your toes facing North. Then you turn clockwise until your toes are pointing in the direction that you want to go.

Bearing 075°   Bearing 215°   Bearing 310°

Use a compass to find North. Your school might have a 'bearings compass' or you might find one on a phone or digital watch. Mark this direction with a ruler or something similar and then try to find the bearing of some objects, for example the garden shed or a lamp-post.

If the bearing is less than 100° you insert a leading zero – all bearings must have three figures.

When you turn around and walk back the way you came, you turn through 180°.
If you have to reverse the direction of a bearing (a 'back bearing'), you simply add 180° to its value.

Bearing	15°	95°	110°	285°
Back bearing	15 + 180 = 195°	95 + 180 = 275°	110 + 180 = 290°	285 + 180 = 465° More than one complete turn so 465 – 360 = 105°

Bearings questions:
- ➤ can ask you to measure accurately or draw angles   (Module 24)
- ➤ can involve angles and parallel lines   (Module 25)
- ➤ can include Pythagoras' theorem and trigonometry.   (Module 32)

Ahab's sat-nav is broken but he has a compass and is sailing North. It is dark and he knows there are dangerous rocks. Coastguards A and B standing on the cliff can see his lights and measure his bearings as 160° and 230°.

Draw bearings and decide if he will hit the rocks if he carries on going North.

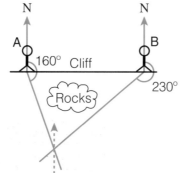

Ahab's position is where the two bearing lines cross. If he keeps going North, he will hit the rocks.

1. The scale of a road atlas is 1 : 250 000
   What do these distances represent in real life (in km)?
   (a) 4cm   **(b)** 10cm   **(c)** 1.5cm
   How far would these distances be on the map (in cm)?
   (d) 35km   **(e)** 40km   **(f)** 5km
2. Draw diagrams to show bearings of
   (a) 085°   **(b)** 190°   **(c)** 300°
   What is the back bearing in each case?

Fractions, decimals and percentages

Per cent means 'out of 100'. There is a direct link between fractions, decimals and percentages.

Fraction	$\frac{n}{100}$	$\frac{1}{100}$	$\frac{50}{100} = \frac{1}{2}$	$\frac{25}{100} = \frac{1}{4}$	$\frac{75}{100} = \frac{3}{4}$	$\frac{10}{100} = \frac{1}{10}$	$\frac{5}{100} = \frac{1}{20}$	$\frac{120}{100} = 1\frac{1}{5}$
Decimal		0.01	0.5	0.25	0.75	0.1	0.05	1.2
Percentage	$n\%$	1%	50%	25%	75%	10%	5%	120%

Calculating with percentages

There are many correct ways to calculate with percentages. The best method often depends whether you are allowed to use a calculator or not.

Three ways to calculate 'increase 480 by 21%' are shown.

Without a calculator	With a calculator	With a calculator and using a multiplier
1% of 480 = 4.8	21% of 480 =	New amount is 121%
10% of 480 = 48	$\frac{21}{100} \times 480 = 100.8$	of original. ← 'of' means '×'
20% of 480 = 96		
480 + 96 + 4.8 = 580.8	480 + 100.8 = 580.8	1.21 × 480 = 580.8

Comparisons using percentages

Percentages allow comparisons to be made easily as everything is written as parts of 100.

If you got 15 in a maths test, you can't tell how well you did unless you know the maximum possible marks. In each case write 15 as a fraction of the total available marks and then write it as a percentage.

$$15 \text{ out of } 20 = \frac{15}{20} = 0.75 = 75\%$$

$$15 \text{ out of } 30 = \frac{15}{30} = 0.5 = 50\%$$

$$15 \text{ out of } 50 = \frac{15}{50} = \frac{30}{100} = 30\% \leftarrow \text{Equivalent fractions}$$

Depreciate ➤ When an object loses value (e.g. cars, motorbikes, computers).

Appreciate ➤ When an object gains value (e.g. property, investments, gold).

Per annum ➤ Per year.

Compound (interest) ➤ The interest earned added so the sum invested increases each year.

KEYWORDS

Percentages and money

An article can **appreciate** (increase) or **depreciate** (decrease) in value by a given percentage.

➤ The value of a painting has appreciated by 15%. If its value **was** £45 000, it is now worth 1.15 × 45 000 = £51 750

➤ The value of a car has depreciated by 15%. If its value **was** £45 000, it is now worth 0.85 × 45 000 = £38 250

   If it lost 15%, it would be now worth 85%

➤ If I bought a mansion for £2.5 million and sold it for £3.2 million:
   My **actual** profit would be £0.7 million or £700 000.
   My **percentage** profit would be
$$\frac{0.7}{2.5} = \frac{7}{25} = \frac{28}{100} = 28\%$$

Module 20 Comparing Quantities

Simple and compound interest

When you invest a sum and then take the interest to spend (perhaps using the interest to live on), this is simple interest. Every year begins with the same sum invested to earn interest.

When you invest a sum and leave the interest in the account (to **compound**), each year the sum is larger and so the interest earned increases. It is easiest to calculate using a multiplier.

Simple	Compound	
£500 at 2% **per annum**	£500 at 2% per annum	Using a multiplier
Y1 $500 \times 0.02 = 10$	Y1 $500 \times 0.02 = 10$	Y3 = $500 \times 1.02^3 = 530.60$
Y2 $500 \times 0.02 = 10$	Y2 $(500 + 10) \times 0.02 = 10.20$	Total interest
Y3 $500 \times 0.02 = 10$	Y3 $(510 + 10.20) \times 0.02 = 10.40$	$530.60 - 500 = £30.60$
Total interest £30	Total interest	
	$10 + 10.20 + 10.40 = £30.60$	

The compound interest principle also applies to repeated depreciation.

If a car worth £10 000 depreciates by 15% per year for five years, then its value is:

$10\,000 \times 0.85^5 = £4437$

It loses 15% so 85% is left.

Make a drink of fruit cordial and measure how much concentrate and how much water you use. Then calculate the percentage of cordial in the drink.

Check the label on the bottle. Can you work out what percentage of your glass contains sugar?

Working backwards

The more difficult questions ask you to work backwards to find a value **before** an increase or decrease. You have to be very careful to read the question correctly, choose your method and show all your steps clearly.

20

A laptop costs £348.50 in a '15% off' sale. What was its price before the sale?

Using %	Using a multiplier
The sale price is 85% of the original. $\dfrac{348.50}{85} = 4.1$ (1% of the original). $4.1 \times 100 = £410$	The sale price is 85% of the original. 85% = 0.85 $\dfrac{348.50}{0.85} = 410$ so £410

A price increase of 8% means a new car is now £27 000. What was its price before the increase?

Using %	Using a multiplier
The new price is 108% of the original. $\dfrac{27\,000}{108} = 250$ (1% of the original). $250 \times 100 = £25\,000$	The new price is 108% of the original. 108% = 1.08 $\dfrac{27\,000}{1.08} = 25\,000$ so £25 000

1. Without a calculator, work out these.
   - (a) 15% of £56
   - (b) Reduce 560 by 30%
   - (c) The value of a £16 000 car after value added tax (VAT) of 20% is added.
2. Using a calculator, work out these.
   - (a) 17% of £112
   - (b) Increase 456 by 27%
   - (c) 42 as a percentage of 520
3. If a plumber's bill was £460.80 after VAT at 20%, what was the price without VAT?

Writing ratios

You can use ratio, using colons (:), to show the proportion between two or more numbers.

If there are 25 dogs and 45 chickens, the ratio of dogs to chickens is

    25 : 45 or

     5 : 9 in its simplest form.   ← Divide both parts by 5.

But the ratio of dogs' feet to chickens' feet is

    100 : 90 or 10 : 9 in its simplest form.

If there are 25 dogs, 45 chickens and 20 sheep, the ratio of dogs : chickens : sheep is

    25 : 45 : 20 or

     5 : 9 : 4 in its simplest form.

Units should be the same when you make comparisons.

£2.50 : 50p as a ratio is 250p : 50p = 5 : 1

5m : 7000cm = 5m : 70m = 1 : 14

Unitary form (1 : n) is most commonly used in maps and scale drawings.

2 : 3 in unitary form is 1 : 1.5

4 : 5 in unitary form is 1 : 1.25

5 : 4 in unitary form is 1 : 0.8

Ratio and fractions

Reducing a ratio to its simplest form is similar to cancelling fractions.

16 : 18 simplifies to 8 : 9   ← Divide both parts by 2.

21 : 28 simplifies to 3 : 4   ← Divide both parts by 7.

There is a link between using ratio and fractions to divide amounts:

Ratio	1 : 2	2 : 3	3 : 5 : 8	1 : 1	1 : 4
Parts / Lots	3	5	16	2	5
Fractions	$\frac{1}{3}, \frac{2}{3}$	$\frac{2}{5}, \frac{3}{5}$	$\frac{3}{16}, \frac{5}{16}, \frac{8}{16}\left(=\frac{1}{2}\right)$	$\frac{1}{2}, \frac{1}{2}$	$\frac{1}{5}, \frac{4}{5}$

Cut out 20 pictures of people, including both children and adults, from a newspaper or magazine. Organise your pictures into two groups – males and females – and write down the ratio of males to females in its simplest form. Then organise the pictures into children and adults and write down the ratio of children to adults in its simplest form.

Using ratio

To divide an amount in a given ratio, you first need to work out how many parts there are in the ratio.

> Divide £840 in the ratio 6 : 5 : 1
>
> There are 6 + 5 + 1 = 12 lots
>
> $\frac{840}{12} = 70$ so 1 lot is £70
>
> 6 × 70 = 420; 5 × 70 = 350; 1 × 70 = 70
>
> So £420 : £350 : £70 ← Check your answer by adding 420 + 350 + 70 = 840

Always read the question carefully.

> Jane and Peter share a basket of apples in the ratio 3 : 5
> If Peter had 15 apples, how many were there altogether?
>
> Peter's apples are 5 parts of the ratio so
> 1 part is $\frac{15}{5}$ = 3 apples.
>
> The whole basket was 8 parts, which is
> 3 × 8 = 24 apples.

There are different ways to compare the value of items.

Which is the best value?

500g £3.50

700g £4.75

For maximum marks, set out your working clearly.

Method 1 Find a price for equal amounts.

Jar A	Jar B
500g cost £3.50	700g cost £4.75
100g cost £0.70	100g cost £0.68

Jar B cheaper for 100g.

Method 2 Find how much you get for an equal price.

Jar A	Jar B
£3.50 buys 500g	£4.75 buys 700g
£1 buys 142.9g	£1 buys 147.4g

£1 buys more with Jar B so Jar B cheaper.

Method 3 Use common multiples.

Jar A	Jar B
500g cost £3.50	700g cost £4.75
× 7	× 5
3500g cost £24.50	3500g cost £23.75

Jar B cheaper for equal amounts.

KEYWORDS

Unitary form ➤ A ratio form involving '1'.

Parts ➤ A ratio divides an amount into a number of equal parts (lots).

1. Peter, Quinn and Robert have been left £44 800. They share it in the ratio of 3 : 5 : 6.
   How much does Quinn get? What fraction of the money does Robert get?
2. Which is the best value for money, 7.5m of ribbon for £6.45 or 5.4m for £4.43?
3. Farmer Jones has 80 chickens. If the ratio of chicken's feet : sheep's foot is 2 : 3, how many sheep does he have?

Direct proportion

When two things are in a constant ratio, they are **directly proportional** ($\propto$) to one another – as one increases so does the other.

There are many examples of direct proportion but the best is probably buying goods. The more bags of cement you buy, the more you will pay.

The total cost (C) is directly proportional to the number of items (n).

Inverse proportion

When two things are **inversely proportional** to one another, one goes up as the other goes down.

Sharing sweets is a good example of inverse proportion.

The more people that share, the fewer sweets they each get.

24 sweets to share: Two people get 12 each or three people get 8 each or twelve people get 2 each.

The number of sweets (s) is inversely proportional to the number of people (p).

22

Expressing proportions

Words	Symbols	Equation (k is a constant)
A is directly proportional to B	$A \propto B$	$A = kB$
A is inversely proportional to B	$A \propto \dfrac{1}{B}$	$A = \dfrac{k}{B}$

Module 22 | Proportion

Solving proportion problems

Variables change in proportion in many areas of maths (and science) including problem-solving, similarity, transformations and trigonometry.

Problem-solving

Temperature (T) is inversely proportional to pressure (P). If T is 5.5 when P is 8, what is T when P is 4?

$$T = \frac{k}{P} \quad \text{so } 5.5 = \frac{k}{8}$$

$$\Rightarrow k = 5.5 \times 8 = 44$$

$$\Rightarrow T = \frac{44}{P}$$

When $P = 4$,

$$T = \frac{44}{4} = 11$$

Similar shapes ← Also see page 62.

Similar shapes

A sheet of A4 paper, when measured to the nearest mm, is 210mm wide by 297mm long. A sheet of A5 is mathematically similar. If it is 148mm wide, what is its length?

Length $\propto$ width so $L = kW$

$$297 = k\,210 \Rightarrow k = \frac{297}{210} = \frac{99}{70}$$

$$\Rightarrow L = \frac{99}{70} W$$

When $W = 148$mm $L = \frac{99}{70} \times 148 = 209$ so 209mm

This problem could also have been solved using ratios.
If the shapes are similar then the ratio between corresponding sides is the same (one is an enlargement of the other).

$$210 : 297$$

$$= 1 : \frac{297}{210} \quad \leftarrow \text{Divide by 210 (leave as a fraction).}$$

$$= 148 : 209 \quad \leftarrow \text{Multiply by 148.}$$

KEYWORDS

$\propto$ ➤ The symbol for 'proportional to'.

Directly proportional ➤ Variables that are in a fixed ratio.

Inversely proportional ➤ As one variable increases, the other decreases.

Cut a sheet of A4 paper in half to make two pieces of A5 size. Cut one A5 piece in half again to make A6. How many A6 pieces would fit on an A4 sheet? If you can find A3 paper then cut that to make A4, A5 and A6. How many A6 sheets would fill one A3 sheet?

1. If 4m of wire costs £6.60, how much will 7m cost?
2. P is proportional to Q and P is 7 when Q is 12. Find the value of P when Q is 6.
3. C is inversely proportional to D. If $C = 9$ when $D = 5$, find D when $C = 3$.

Rates of change and graphs

This graph shows the cost of a mobile phone on three different tariffs.

➤ Line A shows direct proportion. The **gradient** of the line is the rate of change. $\dfrac{\text{change in } y}{\text{change in } x} = \dfrac{10}{40} = 0.25$
This is the constant of proportion and represents the cost per minute of 25p.

➤ Line B shows a fixed charge of £10 before any calls are made. The gradient is $\dfrac{5}{50} = 0.1$
This represents a cost per minute of 10p.

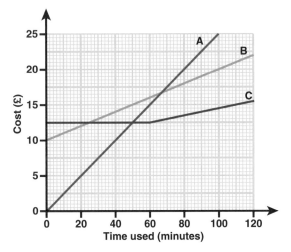

➤ Line C shows a fixed charge of £12.50 and all calls free up to a total of 60 minutes.
After that the gradient is $\dfrac{2.5}{50} = 0.05$
This represents a cost per minute of 5p for all calls after 60 minutes have been used.

You can use this graph to choose which is the best tariff for you. For more than 50 minutes use, C is cheaper, but for low use A is best.

This graph shows Paul's journey from home on foot and by car.

➤ From A to B Paul is walking – he travels 5km in 1 hour.

➤ From B to C Paul is in a car – he travels 20km in 1 hour so his speed is 20km/h.

➤ From C to D Paul is in the same place, perhaps visiting friends.

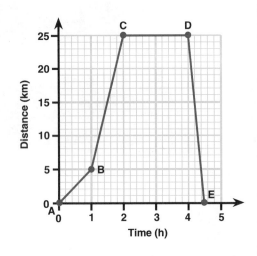

➤ From D to E Paul returns home. He travels 25km in half an hour, so his speed is 50km/h. He finishes his journey back at home.

Take 25 counters (or make your own using pieces of paper). Increase the number of counters by 20%. Increase this number by 40%. Reduce your latest number of counters by 50% and write down how many you are left with.

Inverse proportion graphs

A graph showing inverse proportion looks like this – it is hyperbolic (a **hyperbola**).

Repetitive rates of change

When a percentage change is applied more than once, you must take care to do each step at a time.

A new car costs £23000. In the first year it depreciates by 20%, the next year it loses 15% and then 10% every year after that. To work out the value of the car after three years:

Step-wise
Lose 20% so worth 80%
80% of 23000 = 0.8 × 23000 = 18400
then
85% of 18400 = 0.85 × 18400 = 15640
then
90% of 15640 = 0.9 × 15640 = 14076
Worth £14076 after three years
Using multipliers
Lose 20% so worth 80%
Lose 15% so worth 85%
Lose 10% so worth 90%
0.8 × 0.85 × 0.9 = 0.612
0.612 × £23000 = £14076

1. Work out the gradient of these straight lines.

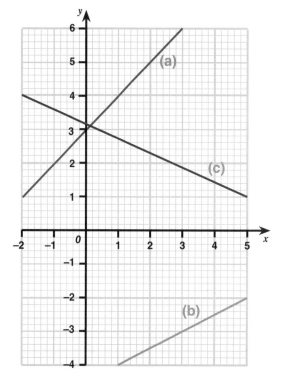

2. These graphs show the height of liquid in a jar as water is poured in at a constant rate.

   Match each graph to the correct container.

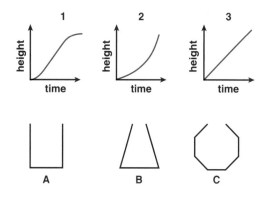

KEYWORDS

Gradient ➤ A numerical value $\dfrac{\text{change in } y}{\text{change in } x}$ that describes the steepness of a line or curve; it can be positive or negative.

Hyperbola ➤ A shape of curve typical of inverse proportion.

Mind Map

Ratio, proportion and rates of change

- Compound interest
- Simple interest
- Percentages
- Ratio
- Fractions
- Scales of maps and drawings
- Scale factors
- Inverse proportion
- Direct proportion
- Rates of change
- Metric measures
- Compound measures
- Graphs
- Gradients of lines and functions

1. Convert 2.5m² to cm². **[2]**

2. Alpha, Beta and Gamma share a legacy in the ratio 3 : 4 : 5

   If Beta had £2400, how much was left to them altogether?

   What fraction of the whole sum did Gamma inherit? **[4]**

3. Amil is buying a computer game on the Internet.

   If the exchange rate is £1 to €1.22, which should he buy? How much will he save?

[3]

4. James and Julia bought a house for £824 000 in 2011. It lost value and they sold it for £760 000 in 2015.

   What was their percentage loss on the transaction? **[2]**

5. A map is drawn using a scale of 1 : 200 000

   Peter measures the motorway distance between junctions 9 and 11 as 9cm.

   (a) What is the actual distance between junctions 9 and 11 in kilometres? **[2]**

   (b) If he drives at an average speed of 90km/h, how many minutes will this part of his journey take him? **[2]**

6. The graph shows the position of a particle over a period of 14 seconds.

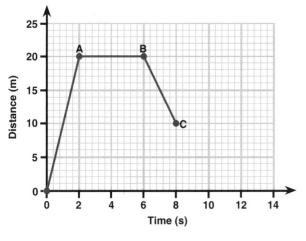

   (a) Find the speed of the particle between 0 and A. **[2]**

   (b) What happens between A and B? **[1]**

   (c) After eight seconds the particle returns to its original position at a speed of 2.5m/s. Complete the graph. **[2]**

Labelling and drawing

You must be able to draw lines of a given length accurately, and use a protractor to draw and measure angles to the nearest degree.

You will see triangles and angles labelled in many different ways.

This triangle could be called triangle *ABC*, *BCA* or *CBA*.

The shaded angle could be correctly called the **acute angle** at *A* or just '*a*':

angle *BAC*   or   angle *CAB*

∠*BAC*   or   ∠*CAB*

BÂC   or   *CÂB*

The side *CA* is extended to *D*.

The **obtuse angle** *DÂB* is an external angle. **Reflex angles** are between 180° and 360°.

Locus

Locus is a Latin word (plural loci) which means location or place. In geometry the locus of a set of points is all the places it can be, according to a given rule.

24

The locus of all points 3cm from the point *C*.	The locus of all points **equidistant** from the **line segment** *AB*.	The locus of all points equidistant from the points *P* and *Q*.	The locus of all points equidistant from the lines *FG* and *GH*.
A circle radius 3cm, centre *C* (or in 3D a sphere).	Two parallel lines joined with semicircles.	The **perpendicular bisector** of the line *PQ*.	The bisector of ∠*FGH*.
			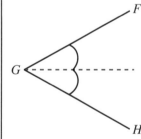

KEYWORDS

Acute angle ➤ An angle between 0° and 90°.

Obtuse angle ➤ An angle between 90° and 180°.

Equidistant ➤ The same distance from.

Line segment ➤ A short section of an infinite line.

Perpendicular to ➤ At 90° to.

Bisector ➤ Divides in half.

Locus/loci ➤ A set or sets of points.

Chalk a line segment on the ground. Using a tape measure or string to help you, chalk the locus of all the points 1 metre from the line segment.

Constructions

Module 24

Accurate constructions

You may have to construct angles and shapes without using a protractor to measure angles. You will only be allowed to use a ruler and a pair of compasses. ← Always leave all the construction arcs for the examiner to see.

You need to know that:
➤ a rhombus has diagonals that bisect its angles
➤ an isosceles triangle has a line of symmetry that bisects the base
➤ an equilateral triangle has all angles = 60°
➤ the shortest distance drawn from a point to a straight line is perpendicular to the line.

1. The locus of all points equidistant from P and Q

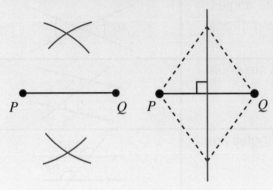

➤ You will construct two isosceles triangles with PQ as the base.
➤ Set compasses to a distance about the same as PQ.
➤ Use arcs to mark the vertices above and below PQ.
➤ Join the vertices – the line is the perpendicular bisector of PQ.

2. The locus of all points equidistant from the lines FG and GH

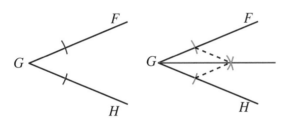

➤ You will draw a line that bisects the angle by constructing a rhombus.
➤ Set compasses to a fixed distance.
➤ From G mark two equal lengths on the lines FG and GH.
➤ Using these marks set the fourth vertex of the rhombus.
➤ Draw the diagonal. This is the angle bisector.

3. Angles of 60° and 30°
➤ Using a pair of compasses and a ruler, construct **any** equilateral triangle. This gives an angle of 60° **without** using a protractor.
➤ To draw 30° you need to bisect the 60° angle. Construct a rhombus – see **2**.

4. Angles of 90° and 45°
➤ Using a pair of compasses, construct a line and its perpendicular bisector to make 90° – see **1**.
➤ To draw 45° you need to bisect the 90° angle. Construct a rhombus – see **2**.

1. Draw the following:
   (a) The locus of all points 3cm from a line of length 5cm.
   (b) The locus of all points equidistant from points S and T which are 6cm apart.
   (c) Two intersecting lines AB and BC and the locus of all points equidistant from both lines.
2. Construct an angle of 30° using a pair of compasses and a ruler only.

Angle rules

25

Look at these angle rules and examples:

Angles at a point	The angles around a point add up to 360°.	107° 32° 221°
Angles on a straight line	The angles along a straight line add up to 180°.	82° 29° 69°
Vertically opposite angles	Vertically opposite angles between two straight lines are equal.	46° 46°
Parallel lines and alternate angles	Alternate angles are equal.	50° 50°
Parallel lines and corresponding angles	Corresponding angles are equal.	130° 130°
Angles in a triangle	Angles in a triangle always add up to 180°.	43° 92° 45°

The properties of triangles

The shape of a triangle is described using its angles and lengths.

Name	Sides	Angles	
Equilateral	Three sides equal; a **regular** triangle	Three angles equal (60°)	Has three lines of symmetry
Isosceles	Two sides equal	Two angles equal	Has one line of symmetry
Scalene	No sides equal	No angles equal	
Right-angled	Could be isosceles or scalene	One right angle	
Obtuse-angled	Could be isosceles or scalene	One obtuse angle	

Proof of angle sum for any triangle

You can use the angle rules to **prove** that the angles inside a triangle always add up to 180°.

$e + b + f = 180°$ (Angles on a straight line sum to 180°.)
angle e = angle a (Alternate angles are equal.)
angle f = angle c (Alternate angles are equal.)
So $a + b + c = 180°$
Angles inside a triangle always add up to 180°.

Cut any triangle out of a sheet of paper. Colour in the angles at the corners and then tear the triangle into three. You will find that you can place the three angles together along a straight edge (they add up to 180°).

KEYWORDS

Parallel ➤ Parallel lines never meet; they can be marked with arrowheads.

Isosceles triangle ➤ A triangle with two equal sides and two equal angles.

Equilateral triangle ➤ A triangle with all sides and angles equal.

Scalene triangle ➤ A triangle with no equal sides or equal angles.

Right-angled triangle ➤ A triangle with one angle of 90°.

1. Find the missing angles, giving your reasons.

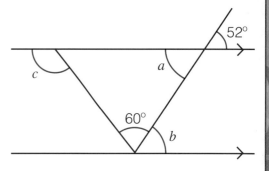

2. Find the angle s.

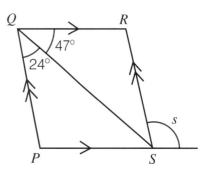

3. Find the angles x, y and z.

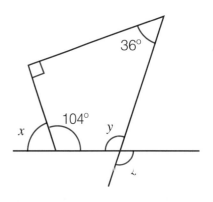

The properties of quadrilaterals

You must know the names of these special quadrilaterals. Quad – four, lateral – side

26

Name	Sides	Symmetry	
Square	Four sides equal Four angles equal (90°) A **regular** quadrilateral	Four lines Rotational order 4	
Rectangle	Two pairs of opposite sides equal Four angles equal (90°)	Two lines Rotational order 2	
Parallelogram	Two pairs of opposite sides equal and parallel (a squashed rectangle)	No lines Rotational order 2	
Rhombus	Four sides equal Two pairs of opposite sides parallel (a squashed square)	Two lines Rotational order 2	
Trapezium	One pair of parallel sides Could also be isosceles	No lines or one line Rotational order 1	
Kite (also a delta or arrowhead)	Two pairs of adjacent sides equal	One line Rotational order 1	

Make any large polygon shape on the floor – you could use metre rules or just mark the corners with books. Start at one corner and walk round your shape, stopping at each corner and turning. This turn is an external angle. When you get back to your start point turn, facing exactly the same way as you started. You will have turned through 360°. The external angles of a polygon add up to 360°, however many sides it has.

Properties of 2D Shapes

Module 26

60 **Module 26** **Properties of 2D Shapes**

The properties of all polygons

Polygons are named by the number of sides.

Sides	3	4	5	6	7	8	9	10
Name	Triangle	Quadrilateral	Pentagon	Hexagon	Heptagon	Octagon	Nonagon	Decagon

A regular polygon has all sides and angles equal. ← A square is a regular quadrilateral.

Polygons have both **external** angles and **internal** angles.

The external angle of any polygon is the angle between one side extended and the next side.

The external angles of any polygon always add up to 360°.

There are two common methods to work out the internal angles in a polygon:

Method 1
➤ Assume the polygon is regular and work out the size of each external angle.
➤ Use the 'angles on a straight line' rule to work out each internal angle.
➤ Calculate the total sum of all the internal angles.

72°

108°

540°

$\frac{360}{5} = 72°$ $180 - 72 = 108°$ $5 \times 108° = 540°$

Method 2
➤ Divide the polygon into triangles.
➤ Use the 'angle sum of a triangle' rule to work out the sum of all the internal angles.
➤ If it is a regular shape, then you can calculate the size of each angle.

180×3
$= 540°$

108°
$\frac{540}{5} = 108°$

---

1. One angle of an isosceles triangle is 62°. Find the other angles. (Note: there are two possible answers.)
2. Sketch an arrowhead (a special sort of kite), which has three of its angles 20°, 80° and 20°.
3. Calculate the external angle of a regular decagon.
4. If the internal angle of a regular polygon is 175°, how many sides has it got?

Similar and congruent shapes

Shapes are **similar** if they have corresponding angles equal and corresponding sides in the same ratio. Shapes are **congruent** if they have corresponding angles and sides equal.

> Congruent shapes are the same shape **and** size.

Conditions for similarity

To show two shapes are similar, you must either:

➤ show that all the corresponding pairs of angles are equal, e.g.

> This would mean that one shape is an enlargement of the other.

or

➤ show that all the corresponding pairs of sides are in the same ratio, e.g.

Conditions for congruency

To prove that two triangles are congruent, you must show that one of the following conditions is true.

> S – side
> A – angle
> R – right angle
> H – hypotenuse

Side–Side–Side (SSS)	Side, Angle, Side (SAS)	Angle, Corresponding Side, Angle (ASA)	Right angle, Hypotenuse, Side (RHS)
All three sides of one triangle are equal to the three sides in the other triangle.	Two sides and the included angle (the angle between them) of one triangle are equal to the two sides and the included angle in the other triangle.	Two angles and a corresponding side of one triangle are equal to two angles and a corresponding side of the other triangle.	Both triangles have a right angle, an equal hypotenuse and another equal side.
			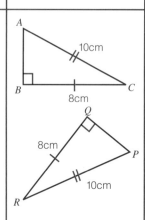
$AB = PQ$, $BC = QR$, $AC = PR$, so congruent (SSS).	$AB = PQ$, $AC = PR$, angle A = angle P, so congruent (SAS).	Angle A = angle P, angle B = angle Q, $BC = QR$, so congruent (ASA).	Angle B = angle Q, $AC = PR$, $BC = QR$, so congruent (RHS).

Proof

You can use congruence to prove angle facts in an isosceles triangle.
An isosceles triangle has two equal sides: $AB = BC$
BD bisects the angle ABC therefore angle ABD = angle CBD
The side BD is common to both triangles.
Therefore SAS: triangle ABD is congruent to triangle CBD
Therefore angle BAD = angle BCD: the base angles are equal.

Create a colourful information poster to show the four conditions of congruency. Accurately draw a pair of triangles to illustrate each condition.

1. Rectangle A has sides 3.4m and 5m. Rectangle B has sides 5.1m and 7.5m. Are the rectangles similar?

2. Are these pairs of triangles congruent? Give your reasons if they are congruent.

(a)

(b)

(c)

(d)

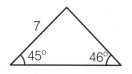

Transformations

All transformations transform an object to make an image. There are four different transformations that you need to know.

Translation

In a translation, every point slides the same distance across the plane. It is described with a **column vector**.

Remember: To describe a translation, you need to state the vector.

Reflection

Every reflection has a **mirror line**. The object is reflected so that the image is reversed and exactly the same distance from the line. ← A mirror image

Remember: To describe a reflection, you need to state the mirror line.

Rotation

Every point in the object is rotated through the same angle about a fixed point.

Remember: To describe a rotation, you need to state the centre of rotation, the angle and the direction.

Enlargement

Enlargement is the only transformation that can give an image which is a different size. The image and the object will always be similar. If the **scale factor** is p, the image of any point will be p times further from the centre of enlargement.

Remember: To describe an enlargement, you need to state the centre of enlargement and the scale factor.

> The image and the object are similar shapes.

Translation	Reflection	Rotation	Enlargement
The vector $\begin{pmatrix} 4 \\ -6 \end{pmatrix}$ translates the object O on to the image I, i.e. the object moves +4 in the x–direction and −6 in the y–direction.	A reflection in the line $x = 1$ moves the object O on to image I.	A rotation of 180° about centre (0, 0) moves the object O on to the image I.	An enlargement of scale factor 2, centre (−2, 0), moves the object O on to the image I.

KEYWORDS

Column vector ➤ A bracket containing values arranged as a column that describe a movement as steps in the x- and the y-directions.

Mirror line ➤ A line used to reflect a shape – it forms a line of symmetry. Points on the mirror line do not move.

Scale factor ➤ The multiplier used to enlarge a shape; the ratio between corresponding sides.

Tricky enlargements

Enlargements can have fractional scale factors:
➤ A scale factor less than 1 gives a smaller image that is closer to the centre of enlargement.

The grid shows O being transformed to I through an enlargement of scale factor $\frac{1}{2}$, centre (0, 0).

Answer the question properly. There is usually a mark for each part of the correct answer.

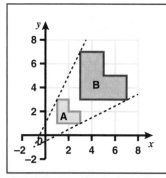

Describe the transformation that moves A on to B.
Enlargement, centre (−1, −1), scale factor 2
or
Describe the transformation that moves B on to A.
Enlargement, centre (−1, −1), scale factor 0.5

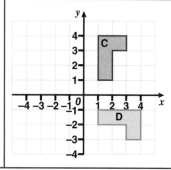

Describe the transformation that moves C on to D.
Rotation, centre (0, 0), 90° clockwise
or
Describe the transformation that moves D on to C.
Rotation, centre (0, 0), 90° anti-clockwise

28

Use a desk light or similar bright light and a pencil to make a shadow on the table. Can you adjust the position of the object (the pencil) to make the image (the shadow) twice as big? Can you get an enlargement of scale factor 3?

1. Describe fully each transformation from green to red.

(a)

(b)

(c)

(d)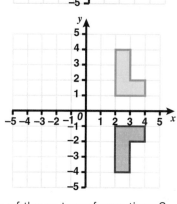

2. What is the **inverse** (opposite) of each of these transformations?
   (a) A reflection in line $y = 2$
   (b) A rotation of 90° clockwise about (2, 1)
   (c) A translation through $\begin{pmatrix} 7 \\ -2 \end{pmatrix}$
   (d) A rotation of 180° about (2, 10)

Circle definitions

You need to know the correct names for the parts of a circle.

The parts of a circle are shown in these diagrams.

Create an information wall using sheets of A3 paper stuck together. Draw two blank circles and use them to illustrate the different parts of a circle.

The circumference and area of a circle

The perimeter of a circle is called the **circumference**.

You will need to remember both formulae for circumference and area.

> Circumference $C = 2\pi r$ or πd
>
> Area $A = \pi r^2$

$C = 2\pi r$ or πd $C = 2 \times \pi \times 3$ $\quad = 6 \times \pi = 18.8m$ (3 s.f.) You can leave your answer 'in terms of π' or you can use your calculator to find a numerical answer.	$C = 2\pi r$ or πd $C = \pi \times 5 = 5\pi$ $\quad = 15.7cm$ (3 s.f.)
$A = \pi r^2 = \pi \times 3^2 = 9\pi m^2$	The radius $r = 5 \div 2 = 2.5cm$ $A = \pi r^2 = \pi \times 2.5^2 = 6.25\pi cm^2$

Be sure to get the units right:

➤ Circumference is a length so the units will be mm, cm, m, km ...
➤ Area is measured in squares so the units will be mm², cm², m², km² ...

KEYWORDS

Circumference ➤ The length of the perimeter of a circle.

Arc ➤ Part of the circumference.

Sector ➤ Part of a circle formed by two radii and an arc (a 'pie slice').

Circles

Module 29

Arcs and sectors

An **arc** is part of the circumference of a circle. A **sector** is a slice of a circle. You use the angle at the centre to work out the fraction of a circle.

The angle is 48°, which is $\frac{48}{360}$ of the whole circle.

So the arc length is $\frac{48}{360} \times 2\pi \times 5 = \frac{4}{3}\pi$ cm

> You should always state the level of rounding you have used.

$= 4.19\text{cm (3 s.f.)}$

The perimeter of the whole sector is the arc plus the two radii $= \frac{4}{3}\pi + 5 + 5\text{cm}$ or 14.2cm (3 s.f.)

The area of this sector is $\frac{48}{360} \times \pi \times 5^2 = \frac{10}{3}\pi\,\text{cm}^2$ or 10.5cm^2 (3 s.f.)

Answering circle questions

Exam questions often include parts of circles. You must be sure what you have to work out. There will be no marks for calculating the area when the question wants the circumference!

A circle question could be on both the non-calculator and calculator papers.

The only difference is how you give your final answer.

12cm

Non-calculator question	Calculator question
Calculate the area. Leave your answer in terms of π.	Calculate the area. Give your answer to 2 significant figures.
Area $= \dfrac{\pi r^2}{2} = \dfrac{\pi \times 6^2}{2}$ $= \dfrac{36 \times \pi}{2}$ $= 18\pi\,\text{cm}^2$	Area $= \dfrac{\pi r^2}{2} = \dfrac{\pi \times 6^2}{2}$ $= \dfrac{36 \times \pi}{2}$ $= 18\pi$ $= 56.5486\ldots = 57\text{cm}^2$ (2 s.f.)

1. Find the area of a circle with diameter 10cm. Leave your answer in terms of π.
2. Find the perimeter of a semicircle with radius 45cm.

   Give your answer to 3 significant figures.
3. Which has the largest area? A circle of radius 4cm or a semicircle of radius 8cm?
4. Find the perimeter and the area of this shaded sector.

3D shapes

A **3D** shape can be described by its **faces**, **edges** and **vertices** (singular 'vertex').

You may have to work out the area of a face. ← 2D measured in square units like cm²

You may have to work out the volume of the whole shape.

3D measured in cubic units like cm³

face ← vertex

edge

Properties of 3D shapes

You need to know, or be able to work out, the properties of these 3D shapes.

	Shape	Name	Vertices	Faces	Edges
Prisms		Cube	8	6	12
		Cuboid	8	6	12
		Cylinder	0	3	2
		Triangular prism	6	5	9
		Hexagonal prism	12	8	18
Pyramids		Tetrahedron	4	4	6
		Square-based pyramid	5	5	8
		Hexagonal-based pyramid	7	7	12
Curved faces		Cone	1	2	1
		Frustum	0	3	2
		Sphere	0	1	0

3D ➤ Three dimensions. An object that has length, width and height.

Face ➤ A polygon that makes one surface of a 3D shape.

Edge ➤ Where two faces meet on a 3D shape.

Vertex ➤ The corner of a 2D or 3D shape.

Plan and elevation

Plans and elevations allow accurate 2D representation of 3D shapes.
They are widely used by architects and designers.
The plan is what you would see if you could hover above the shape – it is the outline.
The elevations are what you would see if you stood beside the shape – they are the outlines.

The Mobius strip – 'every rule has an exception'

Cut a long strip off a sheet of A4 (or larger) stiff paper or card. Twist one short edge by 180° and stick the two short edges together with tape. How many faces and edges has your new shape got? Is it 3D?

1. How many faces, edges and vertices do each of these 3D shapes have?
   (a) A hemisphere
   (b) A pentagonal prism
   (c) A pentagonal-based pyramid

2. Draw the plan and elevations of a hexagonal prism.

3. What shape has a plan and all elevations that are identical circles?

Perimeter, area and volume

Perimeter is a one-dimensional measure. It is a length measured in cm, m, km, inches, miles, etc.

Area is a two-dimensional measure. It is measured in cm², m², km², inches², miles², etc.

Volume is a three-dimensional measure. It is measured in cm³, m³, km³, inches³, miles³, etc.

Perimeter

The perimeter is 'all the way round the edge' so make sure you add up **all** the sides of any shape. Sometimes you will have to calculate a missing length. You must also make sure all the units are the same.

Area

You need to know how to find these areas.

Triangle	Rectangle	Parallelogram	Trapezium	Circle
$A = \frac{1}{2} bh$	$A = bh$	$A = bh$	$A = \frac{1}{2}(a + b)h$	$A = \pi r^2$ (see Module 29)

h is the vertical height, at right angles to the base.

You must make sure all the units are the same and write the correct 'square unit' with your answer.

Find areas of **composite shapes** by chopping them up into any of the simple shapes above.

The two area formulae below are given in your exam, so you will not have to learn them, but you must understand them and be able to use them correctly:

> **Curved surface area of a cone** = πrl (where l is the slant height of the cone)
>
> **Surface area of a sphere** = $4\pi r^2$

A sphere of radius 3cm has surface area $4\pi \times 3^2 = 113\text{cm}^2$ (3 s.f.)

Volume

You need to know how to find these volumes.

Any prism	Any pyramid
Area of the cross-section × height (or length)	$\frac{1}{3}$ area of the base × height
7cm 4cm 3cm	7cm 4cm 3cm
Volume = 3 × 4 × 7 = 84cm³	Volume = $\frac{1}{3}$ × 3 × 4 × 7 = 28cm³

Find more complicated volumes by chopping them up into any of the simple volumes above.

Find the volume of this shape.

Volume of prism = area of cross-section × length

Area of cross-section = 10 × 4 + 4 × 4 ←

$\qquad\qquad\qquad$ = 56cm²   *Split into a rectangle and a square.*

$\qquad$ Volume = 56 × 15 = 840cm³

4cm 4cm
8cm
15cm
10cm

These two volume formulae are given in your exam, so you will not have to learn them, but you must understand them and be able to use them correctly:

Volume of a sphere = $\frac{4}{3}\pi r^3$	**Volume of a cone** = $\frac{1}{3}\pi r^2 h$

Make three larger copies of this net. Fold them to make three identical pyramids that will fit exactly together to make a cube.

KEYWORDS

Composite shape
➤ A shape made up of several different shapes joined together.

---

1. Find the perimeter and area of these shapes.

(a)

10m
4m
4m
3m
3m

(b)

7cm
5cm
12cm
8cm
10cm

2. Find the volume of these shapes.

(a)

4cm
1m
3cm

(b)

20cm
15cm

(c)

16cm
8cm

Pythagoras' theorem

Use Pythagoras' theorem for finding the missing side in a right-angled triangle when you have been given the other two lengths.

$$a^2 + b^2 = c^2$$

The easiest way to remember Pythagoras is using a diagram.

Remember that the squares of the two **short** sides add to give the square of the **longest** side.

Calculate AC.	Calculate PQ.
$a^2 + b^2 = c^2$	$a^2 + b^2 = c^2$
$3^2 + 5^2 = AC^2$	$PQ^2 + 9^2 = 12^2$
$AC^2 = 34$	$PQ^2 = 144 - 81 = 63$
$AC = \sqrt{34}$ cm	$PQ = \sqrt{63}$ m
➤ Non-calculator paper: Leave answer as a square root.	➤ Non-calculator paper: Leave answer as a square root.
➤ Calculator paper: Give rounded decimal answer.	➤ Calculator paper: Give rounded decimal answer.
$AC = \sqrt{34} = 5.83$ cm (3 s.f.)	$PQ = \sqrt{63} = 7.94$ m (3 s.f.)

Basic trigonometry ratios

Basic trigonometry ratios only work for right-angled triangles. They are used to find angles from sides and sides from an angle and a side. Every angle has its own set of sin/cos/tan values.

$$\mathbf{s}\text{ine}\,\theta = \frac{\mathbf{opposite}}{\mathbf{hypotenuse}} \left(\text{s} = \frac{\text{o}}{\text{h}}\right) \quad \mathbf{c}\text{osine}\,\theta = \frac{\mathbf{adjacent}}{\mathbf{hypotenuse}} \left(\text{c} = \frac{\text{a}}{\text{h}}\right) \quad \mathbf{t}\text{angent}\,\theta = \frac{\mathbf{opposite}}{\mathbf{adjacent}} \left(\text{t} = \frac{\text{o}}{\text{a}}\right)$$

> You could learn a mnemonic to help you remember them. Can you make up a better mnemonic than 'SOHCAHTOA'? Silly Old Henry Can…

You need to practise with your calculator.

To solve $a = \sin 45$: key [sin] [4] [5] [=] to get the length $a = 0.707…$

> You may have to close a bracket before hitting [=]

To solve $\sin a = 0.6$: key [sin⁻¹] [0] [.] [6] [=] to get the angle $a = 36.86…°$

> You may have to use the [SHIFT] button to get sin⁻¹.

KEYWORDS

Hypotenuse ➤ The longest side in a right-angled triangle.

Opposite ➤ In a right-angled triangle, the side opposite the angle you are working with.

Adjacent ➤ In a right-angled triangle, the side next to the angle you are working with.

Using trigonometry

Check you can get the correct answers from your calculator for these examples:

Find AB.	Find angle PQR.	Find WX.
		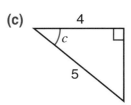
$\text{sine}\,\theta = \dfrac{\text{opposite}}{\text{hypotenuse}}$	$\text{cosine}\,\theta = \dfrac{\text{adjacent}}{\text{hypotenuse}}$	$\text{tangent}\,\theta = \dfrac{\text{opposite}}{\text{adjacent}}$
$\sin 60° = \dfrac{AB}{7.1}$	$\cos PQR = \dfrac{3.5}{4} = \dfrac{7}{8}$	$\tan 43 = \dfrac{2.5}{WX}$
$\Rightarrow AB = 7.1 \times \sin 60$	$PQR = \cos^{-1}\dfrac{7}{8}$	$\Rightarrow WX = \dfrac{2.5}{\tan 43}$
$= 6.15\text{cm}$	$= 29.0°\ (3\,\text{s.f.})$	$= 2.68\text{cm}\ (3\,\text{s.f.})$

Using exact values for sin, cos and tan

Your calculator will give you decimal values of sin, cos and tan but you can also work out exact values for some special angles.

Angle	sin	cos	tan
0°	0	1	0
30°	$\dfrac{1}{2}$	$\dfrac{\sqrt{3}}{2}$	$\dfrac{1}{\sqrt{3}}$
60°	$\dfrac{\sqrt{3}}{2}$	$\dfrac{1}{2}$	$\sqrt{3}$
45°	$\dfrac{1}{\sqrt{2}}$	$\dfrac{1}{\sqrt{2}}$	1
90°	1	0	Does not exist

Draw any right-angled triangle accurately. Draw a square on each side like this. Cut out the two smaller squares. Can you cut them up to fit exactly inside the large square?

---

1. Is a triangle with sides 4.2cm, 7cm and 5.6cm right-angled? Explain your answer.

2. Calculate the missing angles.

    (a)

    (b)

    (c)

3. Calculate the missing lengths.

    (a)

    (b)

    (c)
    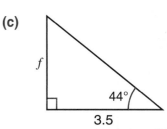

Vectors and translations

A vector can be written as a column vector, as a single bold letter plus an arrow, or with letters and an arrow on the top. It has both length and direction.

On this graph (2, 1) is the fixed point, A.

The column vector $\begin{pmatrix} 1 \\ 3 \end{pmatrix}$ is a **translation** of any point +1 in the x-direction and +3 in the y-direction. On this graph it is the movement from A to C

and can also be written as **a** (with an arrow to show direction) or $\overrightarrow{AC}$.

Working with vectors

You can add and subtract vectors. Think of this as one translation followed by another.

You can multiply any vector by a **scalar** which makes it larger or smaller.

a		$\begin{pmatrix} 1 \\ 2 \end{pmatrix}$
b		$\begin{pmatrix} 2 \\ -3 \end{pmatrix}$
a + b		$\begin{pmatrix} 1 \\ 2 \end{pmatrix} + \begin{pmatrix} 2 \\ -3 \end{pmatrix} = \begin{pmatrix} 3 \\ -1 \end{pmatrix}$
a − b		$\begin{pmatrix} 1 \\ 2 \end{pmatrix} - \begin{pmatrix} 2 \\ -3 \end{pmatrix} = \begin{pmatrix} -1 \\ 5 \end{pmatrix}$
2a		$\begin{pmatrix} 2 \\ 4 \end{pmatrix}$
$\frac{1}{2}$ **b**		$\begin{pmatrix} 1 \\ -1.5 \end{pmatrix}$
2a − b		$\begin{pmatrix} 2 \\ 4 \end{pmatrix} - \begin{pmatrix} 2 \\ -3 \end{pmatrix} = \begin{pmatrix} 0 \\ 7 \end{pmatrix}$

More about vectors

The **inverse** of a vector $\begin{pmatrix} a \\ b \end{pmatrix}$ is the vector $\begin{pmatrix} -a \\ -b \end{pmatrix}$

If you have to describe a vector 'in terms of' other vectors, just find your way between the points using the vectors you already have.

X and Y are the midpoints of AB and AC respectively.

$\overrightarrow{XY} = -\mathbf{a} + \mathbf{b}$ or $\mathbf{b} - \mathbf{a}$ ← [Vectors obey the same rules as numbers.]

$\overrightarrow{YX} = -\mathbf{b} + \mathbf{a}$ or $\mathbf{a} - \mathbf{b}$

$\overrightarrow{AB} = 2\mathbf{a}$ $\overrightarrow{BA} = -2\mathbf{a}$

$\overrightarrow{AC} = 2\mathbf{b}$ $\overrightarrow{CA} = -2\mathbf{b}$

$\overrightarrow{BC} = -2\mathbf{a} + 2\mathbf{b}$

 Use vectors to describe your movement around a room. You will need to decide which is the x-direction and which is the y-direction. For example, $\begin{pmatrix} 3 \\ 4 \end{pmatrix}$ could be three steps to the right and four steps forwards.

Translation ➤ A transformation where every point moves the same amount (a slide).

Scalar ➤ A number (with no units or dimensions).

Inverse ➤ The opposite, e.g. the inverse of +2 is −2 and the inverse of $\begin{pmatrix} 3 \\ -4 \end{pmatrix}$ is $\begin{pmatrix} -3 \\ 4 \end{pmatrix}$.

1. If $\mathbf{p} = \begin{pmatrix} 7 \\ -1 \end{pmatrix}$, $\mathbf{q} = \begin{pmatrix} 2 \\ 2 \end{pmatrix}$ and $\mathbf{r} = \begin{pmatrix} 0 \\ -1 \end{pmatrix}$ calculate:

   (a) $\mathbf{p} + \mathbf{r}$ (b) $\mathbf{p} + \mathbf{q} - \mathbf{r}$
   (c) $3\mathbf{p} + 2\mathbf{q}$ (d) $\mathbf{p} - 2\mathbf{r}$

2. $OABC$ is a quadrilateral, $\overrightarrow{OA} = \mathbf{a}$, $\overrightarrow{OB} = \mathbf{b}$ and $\overrightarrow{OC} = \mathbf{c}$. P, Q, R and S are the midpoints of OA, AB, BC and OC respectively.

Write $\overrightarrow{OP}$, $\overrightarrow{AB}$ and $\overrightarrow{CR}$, in terms of **a**, **b** and **c**.

33

Mind Map

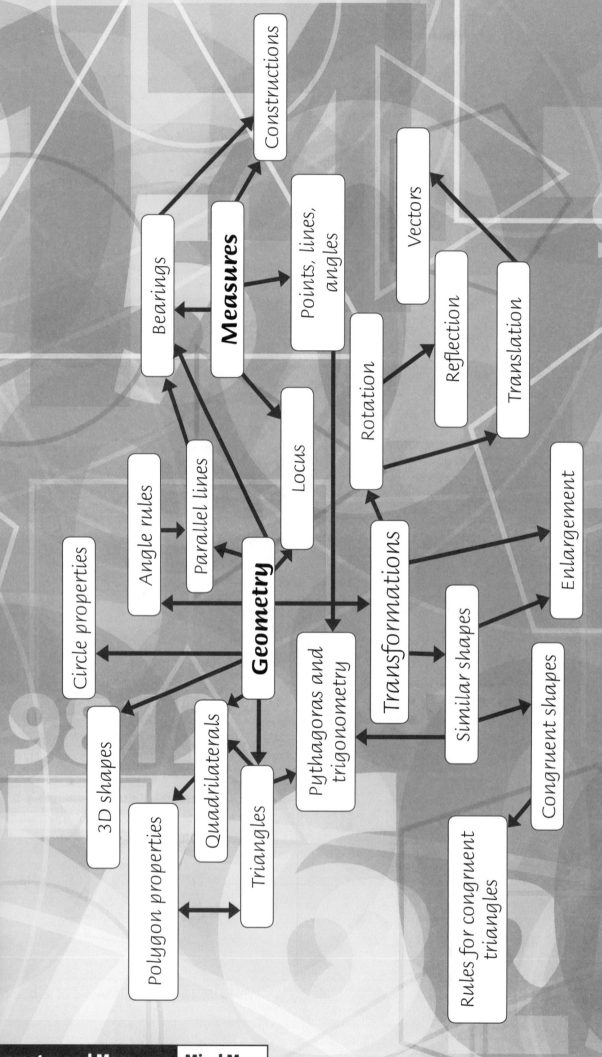

Constructions

Measures

Bearings

Points, lines, angles

Vectors

Reflection

Translation

Rotation

Parallel lines

Angle rules

Locus

Geometry

Circle properties

Transformations

Enlargement

Similar shapes

Pythagoras and trigonometry

Congruent shapes

3D shapes

Quadrilaterals

Triangles

Polygon properties

Rules for congruent triangles

1. If the interior angle of a regular polygon is 156°, how many sides does it have? **[2]**

2. Find the angle *HGD* giving all your reasons. **[3]**

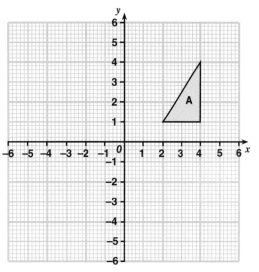

3. In triangle *ABC* the length *AB* = 10cm, angle *BAC* = 92° and angle *ABC* = 20°.
In triangle *RST* the length *SR* = 10cm, angle *RST* = 20° and angle *STR* = 68°.

   Draw triangles *ABC* and *RST* and show that they are congruent, giving your reasons. **[3]**

4. **(a)** Rotate shape A 90° clockwise about the point (0, 0) and label the image B. **[2]**

   (b) Reflect B in the line $x = 0$ and label the image C. **[1]**

5. *OABC* is a parallelogram with *X* the midpoint of *AB* and *Y* the midpoint of *BC*.

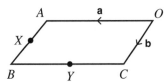

   Use the vectors **a** and **b** to write:

   (a) $\overrightarrow{OA}$ **[1]**   **(b)** $\overrightarrow{OB}$ **[1]**   **(c)** $\overrightarrow{OY}$ **[2]**

6.

   (a) Find the length *NQ*. Give your answer to 2 decimal places. **[3]**

   (b) Find the angle *NMQ*. Give your answer correct to 3 significant figures. **[3]**

7. Find the volume of this cylinder. Give your answer in terms of π. **[3]**

Theoretical probability

Probabilities can be written as fractions, decimals or percentages.
The probability of an event must be between 0 and 1 on the probability scale.

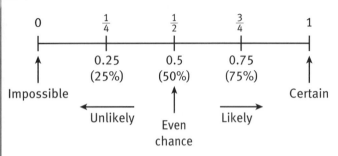

To find the probability of an event, use the formula:

$$P(\text{event}) = \frac{\text{Number of successful outcomes}}{\text{Total number of outcomes}}$$

$P(\text{drawing a king from a deck of cards}) = \dfrac{4}{52}$ ← 4 kings in a deck   ← 52 cards in a deck

Mutually exclusive events

Mutually exclusive events can't happen at the same time. For example, when you roll a dice, you can't get a 1 and a 6 at the same time.

The probabilities of all the outcomes of an event must add up to 1.

The probability of getting each number on a dice is $\frac{1}{6}$ and the probabilities all add up to 1, since it is certain that one of them will occur.

If the probability of event A happening is P, then the probability of event A **not** happening is 1 − P.
P(A) = P   P(not A) = 1 − P

If the probability of a white Christmas is 0.23, then the probability of not having a white Christmas is

$1 - 0.23 = 0.77$ ← The total probability of the two events must equal 1.

KEYWORDS

P(event) ➤ Probability of an event happening.

Mutually exclusive ➤ Events that can't happen at the same time.

Frequency ➤ The number of times something happens.

Biased ➤ Unfair, i.e. weighted on one side.

34

Relative frequency

It is not always possible to calculate a theoretical probability. In such cases the probability can be estimated by doing experiments or trials – this is called relative **frequency**.

This **biased** spinner is spun 20 times and then 100 times. Here are the results:

Score	1	2	3	4	Total trials
First test	2	3	1	14	20
Second test	11	14	7	68	100

$P(4) = \dfrac{14}{20} = 0.7$

$P(4) = \dfrac{68}{100} = 0.68$

The more trials that are done, the more accurate the estimated probability will be. 0.68 is a better estimate than 0.7 for the probability of getting a 4 on this biased spinner.

Expected probability

If the probability of an event is known, then it is easy to predict the number of times that the event is expected to happen. Use the formula:

Expected number of occurrences = Probability of event × Number of trials

The probability that a biased coin will land on heads is 0.24. If the coin is tossed 600 times, how many heads will be expected to occur?

Expected number of heads = 0.24 × 600 = 144

1. A fair dice is rolled. Find:
   (a) P(even)   **(b)** P(prime)   **(c)** P(factor of 6)
2. The probability that a person will pass their driving test is 0.46
   (a) Find the probability that a person will not pass their driving test.
   (b) 500 people take their test this month. How many do you expect to pass?
3. Mary and Max both do an experiment to find out whether a drawing pin will land point up. Mary drops the pin 20 times and Max drops the pin 50 times. Here are the results:

	Point up	Total trials
Mary	13	20
Max	34	50

   (a) Who has the most reliable results and why?
   (b) What is the best estimate for the probability that the pin will land point up?

Roll a dice 30 times and record your results. Do the results show what you would have expected?
Do you believe your dice is biased or fair?

Roll the dice again 60 times and record your results. Are the results now closer to what you would expect?

Sample space

A **sample space** diagram is a list or a table which shows all the possible outcomes of two or more **combined** events.

Two dice are rolled and the scores are added together:

The probability of scoring 9 is $\frac{4}{36}$

Dice 1						
6	7	8	⑨	10	11	12
5	6	7	8	⑨	10	11
4	5	6	7	8	⑨	10
3	4	5	6	7	8	⑨
2	3	4	5	6	7	8
1	2	3	4	5	6	7
	1	**2**	**3**	**4**	**5**	**6**

Dice 2

A meal deal offers a choice of sandwiches plus a snack.

You can choose either a ham (H), cheese (C) or egg (E) sandwich **and** either chocolate (ch) or crisps (cr).

Find the probability that someone at random chooses an egg sandwich and crisps.

You can write all of the outcomes as a list:

(H, ch), (H, cr), (C, ch), (C, cr), (E, ch), (E, cr)

There are exactly six outcomes. Do not write down any repeat outcomes, e.g. (ch, H).

$P(\text{egg and crisps}) = \frac{1}{6}$

Independent events

Independent events can happen at the same time and the occurrence of one event does not affect the occurrence of the other. For example, if you roll a dice and flip a coin, you can get a head and a six and one event does not affect the other.

Learn the following rules:

Rule	What you say	What you do
AND rule	P(A and B)	P(A) × P(B)
OR rule	P(A or B)	P(A) + P(B)

AND means times.

OR means add.

Find the probability of getting a head on a coin and a six on a dice.

$P(\text{head AND six}) = P(\text{head}) \times P(\text{six})$

$$= \frac{1}{2} \times \frac{1}{6} = \frac{1}{12}$$

Tree diagrams

A tree diagram is a useful way of showing all of the outcomes of two or more combined events. They are also an excellent tool for calculating probabilities.

A coin is tossed and the spinner is spun.

Find the probability of getting a head on the coin and an odd number on the spinner.

1st event (coin)	2nd event (spinner)	Final probabilities

Head
- $\frac{2}{3}$ Odd → $\frac{1}{2} \times \frac{2}{3} = \frac{2}{6}$
- $\frac{1}{3}$ Even → $\frac{1}{2} \times \frac{1}{3} = \frac{1}{6}$

Tail
- $\frac{2}{3}$ Odd → $\frac{1}{2} \times \frac{2}{3} = \frac{2}{6}$
- $\frac{1}{3}$ Even → $\frac{1}{2} \times \frac{1}{3} = \frac{1}{6}$

$\frac{1}{2}$ (Head), $\frac{1}{2}$ (Tail)

Total = 1

Multiply across the branches (AND rule).

P(head and odd) $= \frac{2}{6}$

The four different outcomes must add up to 1 (OR rule).

Venn diagrams and set notation

Venn diagrams can also be used to represent and to calculate probabilities.

Some students took a music practical exam and a music theory exam. Everyone passed at least one exam. 46% passed the practical exam and 84% passed the theory exam. Find the probability that a student chosen at random passed the practical exam only.

P(practical exam only) is $\dfrac{16}{100} = 0.16$

46% − 30% = 16%   (84% + 46%) − 100% = 30%   84% − 30% = 54%

This table shows some set notation which is represented by the Venn diagram below.

Set notation	Meaning	Set of numbers
$\mathcal{E} = \{x: 0 < x < 10\}$	Universal set = all items that could occur	{1, 2, 3, 4, 5, 6, 7, 8, 9}
A = $\{x: 0 < x < 10$ and x is odd$\}$	Set A = odd numbers from 0 to 10	Set A = {1, 3, 5, 7 and 9}
B = $\{x: 0 < x < 10$ and x is prime$\}$	Set B = prime numbers from 0 to 10	Set B = {2, 3, 5 and 7}

1.
Two dice are rolled and the scores are added together. Using the sample space diagram on page 80, find:
(a) P(double 6) **(b)** P(not getting a double)
(c) What is the most likely score to occur?

2.
There are 2 black and 3 white counters in a bag. One counter is taken at random, the colour noted and then replaced. A second counter is then taken. Find the probability that both of the counters are black.

Flip a coin three times. Repeat the experiment 40 times. Record the number of times that you get three heads in a row.

Draw a tree diagram for three coins and compare your theoretical results with your experimental results. How close are they?

1. A letter is chosen at random from the word PROBABILITY. Find the probability that the letter will be: 🅕

   (a) A letter B **[1]**   **(b)** A vowel **[1]**

   (c) Not an I **[1]**   **(d)** A letter Q **[1]**

2. The probability that a biased dice will land on the numbers 1 to 5 is given in the table.

Number	1	2	3	4	5	6
Probability	0.1	0.2	0.25	0.1	0.15	

   (a) Find the probability that the dice will land on 6. **[2]**

   (b) The dice is rolled 60 times. How many times do you expect it to land on 5? **[2]**

3. Two fair coins are flipped. Find the probability of getting: 🅕

   (a) Two heads **[2]**

   (b) At least one tail **[2]**

4. A cinema has a £6 food and drink deal. You may choose either a hotdog (D), nachos (N) or popcorn (P) **and** either tea (T), coffee (C), hot chocolate (H) or a soft drink (S).

   (a) Write a list of all the possible outcomes. The first one is done for you:
   (D, T) … **[2]**

   (b) Find the probability that someone at random chooses a hotdog and a coffee. **[2]**

5. Mark and Simon play snooker and then table tennis.
   The probability that Mark will win at snooker is 0.3
   The probability that Mark will win at table tennis is 0.6

   (a) Copy and complete the tree diagram. **[2]**

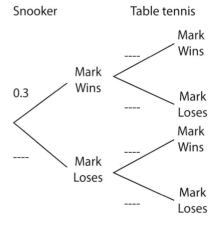

   (b) Find the probability that Mark will win both games. **[2]**

   (c) Find the probability that Mark will win at least one game. **[2]**

6. 50 students were asked to try chocolate A and chocolate B.

   Here are the results: 🅕

   45 said they liked chocolate A   46 said they liked chocolate B   42 said they liked both

   (a) Draw a Venn diagram to show the information. **[2]**

   (b) Find the probability that a student chosen at random did not like either. **[2]**

   (c) Find the probability that a student chosen at random only liked chocolate A. **[1]**

Types of data

You need to know the difference between different types of data.

Averages

There are three types of average – **mean**, **median** and **mode**.
These are used to help compare different **populations**.

Ungrouped data

The table below shows the goals scored by a school football team in 70 games.

Goals scored	Frequency	Total goals	
0	22	0 × 22 =	0
1	21	1 × 21 =	21
2	13	2 × 13 =	26
3	10	3 × 10 =	30
4	2	4 × 2 =	8
5	2	5 × 2 =	10
	70		95

↑ Total number of games

↑ Total number of goals scored in all the 70 games

Mean = $\dfrac{\text{Total goals scored}}{\text{How many games}}$

= 95 ÷ 70 = 1.4 goals per game

Median interval: The group with the middle value. So out of 70 games, halfway is between the 35th and 36th value. Both of these will be in the second group. So the median value is 1.

Mode: Most common number of goals scored is 0 (the group with the highest frequency). So the mode is 0.

Grouped data

The table below shows the times taken by 200 runners in a race.

Time (mins)	Frequency	Midpoint	Frequency × Midpoint
10 ≤ t < 15	1	12.5	12.5
15 ≤ t < 25	8	20	160
25 ≤ t < 35	33	30	990
35 ≤ t < 45	56	40	2240
45 ≤ t < 55	48	50	2400
55 ≤ t < 65	35	60	2100
65 ≤ t < 75	19	70	1330
	200		9232.5

↑ Total number of runners

↑ This is the assumed running time for every person in that group.

↑ Total time taken by all the runners

Estimated mean

= $\dfrac{\text{Total time for all runners}}{\text{How many runners}}$

= 9232.5 ÷ 200 = 46.2 minutes

This is only an estimated mean as it uses the midpoint for each group and not the actual values of the times for each person.

Median interval: Between 100th and 101st runner – both these values will be in the fifth group. So the median will be in the group 45 ≤ t < 55.

Modal group: 35 ≤ t < 45 (the group with the highest frequency)

Module 36 Data and Averages

Sampling

To find out about a population or to test a **hypothesis**, a sample is taken and analysed.

| How has it been collected? Does anything make it biased? | ← | What makes a good sample? | → | Sample size 3 to 10% of the population |

There are different methods of picking a sample (e.g. systematic – pick every tenth one or do it randomly by using a random number generator) and there are different sample types (e.g. stratified – the sample has the same proportion of each group as per the population).

For example, a supermarket chain wants to find out how much people spend on groceries in a week. It asks the first 30 people who shop at its Watford branch in December. This sample would be **biased** as it is limited to one store and so is not a **representative sample**. Also, 30 people is not a large enough sample.

Conduct your own survey on how many text messages people send in a week. Do this for both boys and girls separately. Use a table like this to record your data.

Number of texts	Boys			Girls		
	Freq.	Midpt.	F×M	Freq.	Midpt.	F×M
$0 \leqslant t < 20$						
$20 \leqslant t < 40$						
$40 \leqslant t < 60$						
$60 \leqslant t < 80$						
$80 \leqslant t < 100$						
$100 \leqslant t < 150$						
$150 \leqslant t < 200$						

Create a short video clip on how you calculate the mean for the boys and the mean for the girls.

Two-way tables

Two-way tables show two different variables. Examples include train and bus timetables.

Watford	07.35	08.05	08.35	09.05	10.05
Birmingham	09.25	09.55	10.25	10.55	11.55
Sheffield	10.23	10.53	11.23	11.53	12.23
Leeds	11.36	12.06	12.36	13.06	14.06
Sunderland	12.42	13.12	13.42	14.12	15.12
Newcastle	13.48	14.18	14.48	15.18	16.18

The columns represent the different trains. For example, there is a train leaving Watford at 10.05am and arriving in Leeds at 2.06pm.

KEYWORDS

Discrete data ➤ Can only have set values, e.g. hair colour, shoe size, trouser size.

Continuous data ➤ Can take any value, e.g. things you measure (time, length, weight).

Mean ➤ Total of values divided by the number of values.

Median ➤ The middle value when the data is ordered.

Mode ➤ The most common value.

Population ➤ The data set, e.g. people or objects.

Sampling ➤ A way of collecting data from a population.

Hypothesis ➤ An idea you believe to be true.

1. When working with grouped data, why can you only find an estimate of the mean?
2. Adam has a hypothesis that girls spend more time surfing the Internet than boys. He takes a sample of 10 girls and 10 boys in his class. Is this a good sample? Why?
3. Look at the train timetable (left). Ruth needs to be in Newcastle for an interview at 3.00pm. It will take her 25 minutes to get to the interview from the train station once she arrives. She lives in Sheffield. What is the latest train she can catch and how long will it take?

Pictograms, Venn diagrams, bar charts and line graphs

Pictograms, Venn diagrams, bar charts and vertical line graphs are best for discrete and qualitative data. As well as being able to draw them, you need to be able to read them and pick an appropriate diagram for the situation.

The **pictogram** shows the results of a survey on the different cereals eaten at a school breakfast club.

Key:

⬤ represents 8 people

Half a circle represents 4 people.

Venn diagrams are used to show relationships between sets of data. For example, in the diagram to the right the first set is the number of students who study Geography and the second set is the number of students who study History. The overlap represents the students who study both subjects and the space outside the circles represents students who study neither subject.

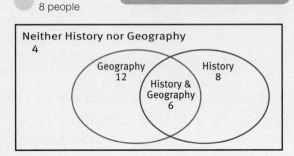

The number of complaints at a call centre was recorded over a period of two weeks.
Bar charts and **line graphs** can be used to compare this data.

Bar chart

	Complaints Week 1	Complaints Week 2
Mon	18	5
Tues	20	12
Wed	12	34
Thurs	10	9
Fri	16	22

Vertical line graph

Pie charts

Pie charts work best for discrete data. Here are the results of a survey of 60 students from Year 7 on how many text messages they send in a week.

This is the number of people in each category.

Number of texts	Frequency	Angle
$0 \leqslant t < 50$	18	$360° \div 60 \times 18 = 108°$
$50 \leqslant t < 100$	20	$360° \div 60 \times 20 = 120°$
$100 \leqslant t < 200$	12	$360° \div 60 \times 12 = 72°$
$200 \leqslant t < 300$	10	$360° \div 60 \times 10 = 60°$

Remember that there are 360° in a circle. So divide 360 by the total frequency (60 students), then multiply by the frequency for each category.

Survey of Year 7 students – text messages sent per week

- $0 \leqslant t < 50$
- $50 \leqslant t < 100$
- $100 \leqslant t < 200$
- $200 \leqslant t < 300$

Line graphs for time series data

Some types of data that are measured against time can be represented on a time series graph. Examples include prices, Retail Price Index, share prices, sales, etc. You will need to be able to plot and interpret these.

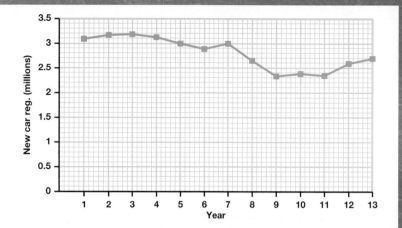

Scatter graphs

Scatter graphs are used to test for a relationship between two variables. They will show positive **correlation**, negative correlation or no correlation.

Create your own pie chart on an A4 sheet of paper to show the number of pages in 40 books in your home. You might group the books into categories of 0–50 pages, 51–100 pages, 101–200 pages, 201–300 pages, 301 or more pages, etc.

For positive and negative correlations, a line of best fit is drawn through the centre of all the points.

There is a point which does not fit the trend at all. It is known as an **outlier**.

37

A correlation can be weak or strong, depending on how closely the points follow the line of best fit. You can use a line of best fit to make predictions but only **within the range of the data**. It would be unreliable to extend the line of best fit and make predictions beyond the range of the data because the relationship may not hold.

1. Look at the time series graph above.
   (a) What could have caused the dip in years 7–9 in new car registrations?
   (b) How many new car registrations would you predict for year 14?

Comparing data

When comparing data you will be expected to be able to interpret any of the diagrams in Module 37, as well as use the averages and the range to compare distributions.

Measures of central tendency – the averages

Consider the scores below for a maths test:

23   10   34   21   41   39   23   34   30   22   34   32

Putting this data in order: 10, 21, 22, 23, 23, 30, 32, 34, 34, 34, 39, 41 ←

> The mean will lie somewhere within the range of this data, so it will not be less than 10 and it will be no more than 41.

Mean: 343 ÷ 12 = 28.6

> Total of test scores

> Number of scores in the data

Mode: 34 ← The test score that occurs most times.

Median: 31 ← The score that represents the middle value when the data is ordered. In this case, the median lies between the sixth and seventh values because there is an even number of test scores in the data.

Range: 41 – 10 = 31 ← Maximum test score – Minimum test score

Consider what happens to the averages when you add an outlier to the data:

10, 21, 22, 23, 23, 30, 32, 34, 34, 34, 39, 41, (95)

Mean is now 438 ÷ 13 = 33.7 ← Higher than before   Mode is 34 ← No change

Median is now the seventh value = 32 ← Small change   Range is now 95 – 10 = 85 ← Big change

Average	Advantage	Disadvantage
Mean	Uses every value so represents all the data	Affected by outliers (extreme values)
Median	Not affected by outliers	Only represents a single value in the middle of the distribution
Mode	Used for numbers and words; not affected by outliers	Limited use
Range	Gives a guide on how spread out the distribution is	Only uses minimum and maximum values and can be highly affected by outliers

Comparing distributions from a list

In a survey of gym members, the time (in hours) spent exercising in a week was recorded.

Male:	8	15	7	7	6	8	9	6	6	5
Female:	2	6	5	6	5	3	4	4	6	2

	Male	Female
Mean	77 ÷ 10 = 7.7	43 ÷ 10 = 4.3
Mode	6	6
Median	(7 + 7) ÷ 2 = 7	(4 + 5) ÷ 2 = 4.5
Range	15 – 5 = 10	6 – 2 = 4

← Mean suggests that males spend much longer exercising than females (7.7 vs 4.3 hours).

← Mode for both groups is the same.

← Medians also suggests that males spend longer exercising (7 vs 4.5 hours).

Looking at the spread of the two distributions, the presence of the outlier gives a much higher range for the males (10 vs 4 hours). Care must be taken as the majority of the males spent between 5 and 9 hours exercising and some of the females were in this range.

Module 38   Comparing Distributions

Comparing distributions from a table

The pay and equal rights service monitors the differences in men and women's pay. It conducted a survey of male and female salaries for physiotherapists.

For men:

Salary (£)	Frequency
0 < £ ≤ 15 000	1
15 000 < £ ≤ 20 000	8
20 000 < £ ≤ 25 000	20
25 000 < £ ≤ 30 000	16
30 000 < £ ≤ 50 000	5

Estimated mean: 1 237 500 ÷ 50 = £24 750

Modal group: 20 000 < £ ≤ 25 000

Median interval: 20 000 < £ ≤ 25 000 (25th/26th value will be in this group)

For women:

Salary (£)	Frequency
0 < £ ≤ 15 000	3
15 000 < £ ≤ 20 000	5
20 000 < £ ≤ 25 000	18
25 000 < £ ≤ 30 000	22
30 000 < £ ≤ 50 000	2

Estimated mean: 1 200 000 ÷ 50 = £24 000

Modal group: 25 000 < £ ≤ 30 000

Median interval: 20 000 < £ ≤ 25 000 (25th/26th value will be in this group)

So do women get paid less than men? Give reasons for your answer.

Comparing the two sets of data:
- The mean is slightly higher for men (£24 750 vs £24 000), which suggests they get paid more.
- The modal group for men is lower (20 000 < £ ≤ 25 000 vs 25 000 < £ ≤ 30 000), which suggests women get paid more.
- The median for both groups is 20 000 < £ ≤ 25 000.

It is difficult to give a clear case for either but, overall, as the mean includes all the data, the survey suggests that men do get paid more than women.

Create flashcards to make sure you know the meaning of all the keywords in Modules 36 to 38. Write the keyword on one side of the flashcard and the definition on the other. Write definitions using your own words but make sure they are accurate by checking against this book.

1. Which of these can be significantly distorted by an outlier?
   Mean   Median   Mode   Range
2. The results of an analysis on the daily sales for two different stores are summarised in the table below. Which store has the best sales?

	Store A	Store B
Estimate of the mean	£3400	£3900
Modal group	2000 < £ ≤ 3000	3000 < £ ≤ 4000
Interval containing the median	2000 < £ ≤ 3000	2000 < £ ≤ 3000

Statistics

Mind Map

Secondary

Primary

Discrete

Two-way tables

Continuous

Ungrouped

Data

Pictograms
Venn diagrams
Pie charts
Bar charts
Vertical line graphs

Time series

Compare distributions

Statistics

Statistical diagrams

Outlier

Scatter graphs

Correlation

Line of best fit

Outliers

Averages

Mode

Median

Mean

Grouped (estimated mean)

1. In a survey of cinema-goers, 10 people said they liked Horror, 18 people said they liked Romance, 15 people said they liked Sci-Fi and 8 liked Thrillers.

   Show this data on a pictogram. **[3]**

2. A sales manager wants to compare the sales figures for May–October against the same period the previous year. Draw a suitable diagram to represent this data.

	Sales Year 1 (k)	Sales Year 2 (k)
May	11	6
June	17	12
July	26	18
August	34	25
September	16	12
October	5	6

   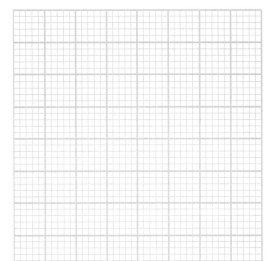

   [3]

3. Look at this data showing the weights of 200 people.

Weight (w kg)	Frequency
$10 \leqslant w < 15$	36
$15 \leqslant w < 25$	24
$25 \leqslant w < 35$	13
$35 \leqslant w < 45$	31
$45 \leqslant w < 55$	40
$55 \leqslant w < 65$	33
$65 \leqslant w < 75$	23
	200

   Find:
   (a) an estimate of the mean **[4]**
   (b) the median interval **[1]**
   (c) the modal group **[1]**

4. Five positive integers have a median of 5, a mean of 6 and a mode of 3.
   What is the greatest possible range for the numbers? **[3]**

Module 1 – Place Value and Ordering

1. (a) +3   (b) –8   (c) –5
2. (a) 48   (b) –8   (c) –60
3. (a) False   (b) True   (c) True
4. (a) 2.451   (b) 245 100   (c) 430

Module 2 – Factors, Multiples and Primes

1. (a) Factors of 12: 1, 2, 3, 4, 6, 12   Factors of 15: 1, 3, 5, 15
   (b) 3
2. (a) 7, 14, 21, 28, 35, 42, 49, 56   5, 10, 15, 20, 25, 30, 35, 40
   (b) 35
3. (a) $28 = 2 \times 2 \times 7$ $98 = 2 \times 7 \times 7$
   (b) $28 = 2^2 \times 7$ $98 = 2 \times 7^2$
   (c) HCF = 14   LCM = 196

Module 3 – Operations

1. (a) 18   (b) 24   (c) 38   (d) 2
2. (a) $\dfrac{5}{2}$ (b) 7   (c) $\dfrac{1}{5}$ (d) 4
3. (a) $\dfrac{1}{20}$ (b) $5\dfrac{5}{8}$ (c) $\dfrac{20}{21}$ (d) $4\dfrac{2}{3}$

Module 4 – Powers and Roots

1. (a) 4^3 (b) 3^5 (c) 2^{-3}
2. (a) (i) 3^9 (ii) 4^7 (iii) 6^7
   (b) (i) 1   (ii) $\dfrac{1}{125}$ (iii) 2
3. (a) (i) 6×10^3 (ii) 2.3×10^3 (iii) 6.78×10^{-3}
   (iv) 1.5×10^{-1}
   (b) (i) 1.8×10^{10} (ii) 2×10^6 (iii) 4.71×10^6

Module 5 – Fractions, Decimals and Percentages

1. (a) 0.6   (b) 0.875   (c) 0.6666…   (d) 0.65
2. (a) $\dfrac{9}{25}$ (b) $\dfrac{31}{125}$ (c) $\dfrac{2}{25}$
3. (a) 30.87   (b) 30   (c) 14.4

Module 6 – Approximations

1. (a) 38   (b) 370   (c) 400   (d) 5000
2. (a) 2.39   (b) 4.610   (c) 44 000   (d) 0.004 03
3. 750
4. (a) $22.5\,\text{m} \leqslant x < 23.5\,\text{m}$ (b) $4.65\,\text{kg} \leqslant x < 4.75\,\text{kg}$
   (c) $5.225\,\text{km} \leqslant x < 5.235\,\text{km}$

Module 7 – Answers Using Technology

1. (a) 12.167   (b) 4096   (c) 8
2. 3.1666…
3. (a) 9.88×10^3 (b) 7.46×10^{14}

Module 8 – Algebraic Notation

1. (a) $12ab + 2a^2b$
   (b) $9x - 9$
   (c) $2ab + 2ac + 2bc$
2. (a) g^8
   (b) p^5
   (c) $14p^2q^{-2}$
3. (a) 4
   (b) $\dfrac{1}{16}$
   (c) $\dfrac{27}{8}$

Module 9 – Algebraic Expressions

1. (a) $10 - 15x$
   (b) $x^2 - 2x - 35$
2. (a) $(x + 7)(x - 8)$
   (b) $(2p + 5q)(2p - 5q)$
3. (a) $2x^2 + x - 3$
   (b) $9x^2 - y^2$

Module 10 – Algebraic Formulae

1. (a) $p = \dfrac{b - a}{3}$
   (b) $p = \dfrac{2 - 3q}{2q - 3}$
2. (a) $p = 84$
   (b) $p = -\dfrac{3}{10}$
3. (a) $3x + x - 2 + 2x - 10 = 180$
   (b) $x = 32°$
   (c) 96°, 30°, 54°

Module 11 – Algebraic Equations

1. (a) $x = 7$ (b) $x = \dfrac{1}{3}$
2. $x = 10, x = 1$
3. $x = 2, y = -5$
4. $x = 5$

Module 12 – Algebraic Inequalities

1. (a) $x < 8$ (b) $x \leqslant -2.5$
2. (a) $x > -3$ (b) $x \leqslant 2$
3. $x < \dfrac{8}{3}$

$\dfrac{8}{3}$

Module 13 – Sequences

1. 0, 3.5, 13
2. (a) $U_n = 9n - 5$
   (b) 895
   (c) No, since $9n - 5 = 779$ has no integer solution.

Module 14 – Coordinates and Linear Functions

1. $y = 3x - 2$
2. $y = 2x + 16$ and $4y = 8x - 1$
3. $y = 4x - 32$
4. $9x - 4y - 6 = 0$ or $y = \dfrac{9}{4}x - \dfrac{3}{2}$

Module 15 – Quadratic Functions

1. (a) (–5, 0), (8, 0)
   (b) (0, –40)
   (c) $x = \dfrac{3}{2}$
2. (a) $x = -5$ (b) (–5, –65)

Module 16 – Other Functions

1. Output $f(x) = 6, 5, 4, 3$
2. $f(x) = 2x + 5$

3. $f(x) = \dfrac{2}{x}$

$f(x) = \dfrac{1}{x}$

$f(x) = \dfrac{-2}{x}$

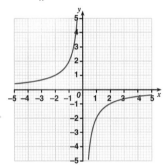

Module 17 – Problems and Graphs
1. A 2
   B 5
   C 4
   D 1
   E 3
2. **(a)** 5 seconds **(b)** 2m/s² **(c)** 200m

Module 18 – Converting Measurements
1. 17.8m/s (3 s.f.) **2.** In UK €80 = £64 or £48 = €60
3. 84cm² **4.** 2 500 000cm³

Module 19 – Scales, Diagrams and Maps
1. **(a)** 10km **(b)** 25km **(c)** 3.75km
   (d) 14cm **(e)** 16cm **(f)** 2cm
2. Accurately drawn diagrams to ±1°.
   (a) 265° **(b)** 010° **(c)** 120°

Module 20 – Comparing Quantities
1. **(a)** £8.40 **(b)** 392 **(c)** £19 200
2. **(a)** £19.04 **(b)** 579.12 **(c)** 8.1% (2 s.f.)
3. £384

Module 21 – Ratio
1. £16 000, $\dfrac{3}{7}$ **2.** 5.4m for £4.43 (82 p/m and 86 p/m) **3.** 60

Module 22 – Proportion
1. £11.55 **2.** 3.5 **3.** 15

Module 23 – Rates of Change
1. **(a)** 1 **(b)** 0.5 **(c)** $-\dfrac{3}{7}$
2. Graph 1 — C; Graph 2 — B; Graph 3 — A

Module 24 – Constructions
1. **(a)** Two lines parallel to and 3cm away from the drawn line (above and below), joined with semicircles of radius 3cm at each end
   (b) Accurate perpendicular bisector of line *ST*
   (c) Accurate angle bisector
2. Accurate 60° angle with visible construction lines and angle bisector

Module 25 – Angles
1. $a = 52°$ (opposite angles), $b = 52°$ (corresponding / alternate angles), $c = 112°$ (alternate to 60° + 52°)
2. 109° **3.** $x = 76°$, $y = 130°$, $z = 130°$

Module 26 – Properties of 2D Shapes
1. Either 62°, 56° or 59°, 59° **2.** Missing angle 240°
3. 36° **4.** 72

Module 27 – Congruence and Similarity
1. Yes (ratios both 1.5)
2. **(a)** Yes SAS or ASA **(b)** Yes ASA **(c)** Yes RHS **(d)** No

Module 28 – Transformations
1. **(a)** Translation $\begin{pmatrix} -1 \\ -5 \end{pmatrix}$
   (b) A rotation of 90° clockwise about (0, 0)
   (c) Translation $\begin{pmatrix} 0 \\ -5 \end{pmatrix}$
   (d) A reflection in line $y = 0$ (or the *x*-axis)
2. **(a)** A reflection in line $y = 2$
   (b) A rotation of 270° clockwise or 90° anti-clockwise about (2, 1)
   (c) A translation through $\begin{pmatrix} -7 \\ 2 \end{pmatrix}$
   (d) A rotation of 180° about (2, 10)

Module 29 – Circles
1. 25πcm²
2. 231cm
3. Semicircle (circle = 16π and semicircle = 32π)
4. $\dfrac{40}{3}$ π + 15 or 56.9cm (3 s.f.); 50π or 157cm² (3 s.f.)

Module 30 – Properties of 3D Shapes
1. **(a)** 2 faces, 1 edge, 0 vertices
   (b) 7 faces, 15 edges, 10 vertices
   (c) 6 faces, 10 edges, 6 vertices
2. Any suitable answer, e.g.

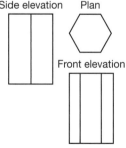

3. A sphere

Module 31 – Perimeter, Area and Volume
1. **(a)** 34m, 28m²   **(b)** 42cm, 114cm²
2. **(a)** 600cm³   **(b)** 1500π or 4712cm³ (4 s.f.)
   (c) 504π or 1583cm³ (4 s.f.)

Module 32 – Pythagoras' Theorem and Trigonometry
1. Yes. $4.2^2 + 5.6^2 = 7^2$ Pythagoras' theorem holds therefore right-angled.
2. **(a)** 40.6° (3 s.f.)   **(b)** 58.4° (3 s.f.)   **(c)** 36.9° (3 s.f.)
3. **(a)** 6.11 (3 s.f.)   **(b)** 3.66 (3 s.f.)   **(c)** 3.38 (3 s.f.)

Module 33 – Vectors
1. **(a)** $\begin{pmatrix} 7 \\ -2 \end{pmatrix}$ **(b)** $\begin{pmatrix} 9 \\ 2 \end{pmatrix}$ **(c)** $\begin{pmatrix} 25 \\ 1 \end{pmatrix}$ **(d)** $\begin{pmatrix} 7 \\ 1 \end{pmatrix}$
2. $\overrightarrow{OP} = \frac{1}{2}\mathbf{a}$, $\overrightarrow{AB} = -\mathbf{a} + \mathbf{b}$, $\overrightarrow{CR} = \frac{1}{2}(\mathbf{b} - \mathbf{c})$

Module 34 – Experimental and Theoretical Probability
1. **(a)** $\frac{3}{6}$ or $\frac{1}{2}$
   (b) $\frac{3}{6}$ or $\frac{1}{2}$
   (c) $\frac{4}{6}$ or $\frac{2}{3}$
2. **(a)** 0.54   **(b)** 230
3. **(a)** Max, because he has done more trials.
   (b) $\frac{47}{70}$

Module 35 – Representing Probability
1. **(a)** $\frac{1}{36}$ **(b)** $\frac{30}{36}$ or $\frac{5}{6}$ **(c)** 7
2. $\frac{4}{25}$

Module 36 – Data and Averages
1. Because it is assumed each value is at the midpoint for each group when calculating the mean.
2. No. Needs to use a bigger sample and ask a variety of boys and girls of different ages.
3. 10.53, 3h 25 mins

Module 37 – Statistical Diagrams
1. **(a)** Any suitable answer, e.g. Slowdown in people's spending, recession, increases in prices/tax.
   (b) On an upward trend, so anything in the range 2.7–3.2 million.

Module 38 – Comparing Distributions
1. Mean and range
2. Store B as it has a higher estimated mean (£3900 vs £3400) and a higher modal group (3000 < £ ≤ 4000 vs 2000 < £ ≤ 3000)

Exam Practice Questions
Number
1. **(a)** 4 × 58 = 232 **[1]**   23.2 **[1]**
   (b) 23 × 427 = 9821 **[2]** (use long multiplication)   98.21 **[1]**
   (c) 2400 ÷ 8 **[1]** (multiply both figures by 100) = 300 **[1]**
   (d) 468 ÷ 36 **[1]** (multiply both figures by 10, then long division) = 13 **[1]**
   (e) −7 **[1]**
   (f) −3 **[1]**
   (g) −5 **[1]**
   (h) −140 **[1]**
   (i) 4 + 63 = 67 **[1]**
   (j) −31 − 9 **[1]** = −40 **[1]**

2. **(a)** 36 = 2 × 2 × 3 × 3 **[1]** (use factor trees) = $2^2 \times 3^2$ **[1]**
   (b) 48 = 2 × 2 × 2 × 2 × 3 **[1]** (use factor trees) = $2^4 \times 3$ **[1]**
   (c) HCF = 2 × 2 × 3 **[1]** (the common prime factors) = 12 **[1]**
   (d) LCM = 12 × 2 × 2 × 3 **[1]** (HCF multiplied by the remaining prime factors) = 144 **[1]**
3. **(a)** $\frac{4 \times 5}{3 \times 6}$ **[1]** $= \frac{20}{18} = \frac{10}{9} = 1\frac{1}{9}$ **[1]**
   (b) $7\frac{11}{12} - (2\frac{3}{4} + 3\frac{5}{6})$ **[1]** $= 7\frac{11}{12} - (6\frac{7}{12})$ **[1]** $= 1\frac{1}{3}$ **[1]**
   (c) $\frac{16}{5} \times \frac{4}{9}$ **[1]** $= \frac{64}{45}$ **[1]** (convert to improper fractions, flip second fraction and multiply) = $1\frac{19}{45}$ **[1]**
4. **(a)** $5^{3--5} = 5^8$ **[1]**
   (b) $3^{(4+8+1)} = 3^{13}$ **[1]**
   (c) $\frac{7^7}{7^3}$ **[1]** $= 7^4$ **[1]**
5. **(a)** 1 **[1]**
   (b) 5 × 5 × 5 × 5 = 625 **[1]**
   (c) $\frac{1}{3^2}$ **[1]** $= \frac{1}{9}$ **[1]**
6. **(a) (i)** 6.7×10^7 **[1]**   **(ii)** 7×10^{-6} **[1]**
      (iii) 4.36×10^4 **[1]**   **(iv)** 8.03×10^{-3} **[1]**
   (b) (i) 12×10^{11} **[1]**
         (put back into standard form) = 1.2×10^{12} **[1]**
      (ii) 0.021 + 0.0057 = 0.0267 **[1]**
         (put back into standard form) = 2.67×10^{-2} **[1]**
      (iii) $(1.2 \div 3) \times (10^{8-4})$ **[1]** $= 0.4 \times 10^4 = 4 \times 10^3$ **[1]**
7. **(a)** $5.5\,\mathrm{m} \leqslant x < 6.5\,\mathrm{m}$
   (b) $5.45\,\mathrm{m} \leqslant x < 5.55\,\mathrm{m}$

Algebra
1. **(a)** $3x − 6 − 4x + 4 = 0$ **[1]** $x = −2$ **[1]**
   (b) $5(x + 8) = 3(2x − 9)$ **[1]** $5x + 40 = 6x − 27$ **[1]** $x = 67$ **[1]**
2. A and C are parallel. **[2]**
3. $S = 12$ **[2]**
4. $6a(3a − b)$ **[2]**
5. **(a)** $x = −1.5$, $x = 2$ **[2]**   **(b)** (0, 6) **[1]**
   (c) $x = \frac{1}{4}$ **[1]**
6. **(a)** $(x + 9)(x + 7) = 0$ **[1]**
      $x + 9 = 0$ or $x + 7 = 0$
      $x = −9$ or $x = −7$ **[2]**
   (b) $(x + 10)(x − 3) = 0$ **[1]**
      $x + 10 = 0$ or $x − 3 = 0$
      $x = −10$ **[1]** or
      $x = 3$ **[1]**
7. 185 **[2]**
8. $y(x − 2) = 3x + 1$
   $yx − 2y = 3x + 1$ **[1]**
   $yx − 3x = 2y + 1$
   $x(y − 3) = 2y + 1$ **[1]**
   $x = \frac{2y + 1}{y − 3}$ **[1]**
9. $6x + 9y = 3$
   $6x − 4y = −36$ **[2]**
   $13y = 39$
   $y = 3$ **[1]**
   $x = −4$ **[1]**
10. **(a)**

[2]

(b) Attempt to divide through by x **[1]**

$x + 1 = \dfrac{4}{x}$ **[1]**

So plot $y = x + 1$ **[1]**

Ratio, Proportion and Rates of Change

1. $2.5 \times 100 \times 100$ **[1]** $= 25\,000\,cm^2$ **[1]**
2. $2400 \div 4$ **[1]** $= 600$

   $600 \times (3 + 4 + 5)$ **[1]** $= £7200$ **[1]**

   $\dfrac{5}{12}$ **[1]**
3. $77 \div 1.22$ or $£64 \times 1.22$ **[1]**

   Game for 77 euros is cheaper **[1]** by 89 p or €1.08 **[1]**
4. $\dfrac{824\,000 - 760\,000}{824\,000}$ or $\dfrac{64\,000}{824\,000}$ **[1]** $= 0.078$

   7.8% **[1]**
5. **(a)** $9 \times 200\,000$ **[1]** $= 1\,800\,000\,cm = 18km$ **[1]**

   (b) $\dfrac{18}{90} = \dfrac{1}{5}$ or 0.2 **[1]** $h = 12$ minutes **[1]**
6. **(a)** $\dfrac{20}{2}$ **[1]** $= 10m/s$ **[1]**

   (b) The particle is stationary **[1]**.

   (c) Line drawn from C to point (12, 0) **[1 if fully correct; 1 for any straight line from C to time axis beyond $t = 8$]**

Geometry and Measures

1. Exterior angle $180 - 156$ **[1]** $= 24°$ $\dfrac{360}{24} = 15$ **[1]**
2. Example answer: Angle $BHG = 180 - (46 + 92)$ **[1]**

   $= 42°$ (angles on straight line add up to 180°)

   Angle $HGC = 42°$ (alternate angles are equal)

   Angle $HGD = 180 - 42 = 138°$ (angles on straight line add up to 180°) **[1]**

   All reasons correct **[1]**
3. Angle $SRT = 180 - (20 + 68) = 92°$ **[1]**

   Diagram **[1]** ASA so congruent **[1]**
4. **(a)** Any rotation **[1]**, (1, −2), (1, −4), (4, −4) **[1]**

   (b) Correct reflection of the rotated image to (−1, −2), (−1, −4), (−4, −4) **[1]**
5. **(a)** **a** **[1]**   **(b)** **a** + **b** **[1]**

   (c) $\overrightarrow{CY} = \dfrac{1}{2}$ **a** **[1]**, so $\overrightarrow{OY} = \dfrac{1}{2}$ **a** + **b** **[1]**
6. **(a)** $NQ^2 + 4^2 = 6^2$ **[1]**

   $NQ^2 = 20$ **[1]**

   $NQ = 4.47cm$ **[1]**

   (b) $NQ = \sqrt{NP^2 - QP^2} = \sqrt{6^2 - 4^2}$ **[1]**

   $NQ = \sqrt{20}$ $\sin M = \dfrac{\sqrt{20}}{7}$ **[1]** $= 0.6389$

   $M = 39.7°$ **[1]**
7. Radius = 4cm **[1]**

   Volume $= \pi \times 4^2 \times 10$ **[1]**

   $= 160\pi\,cm^3$ **[1]**

Probability

1. **(a)** $\dfrac{2}{11}$ **[1]**

   (b) $\dfrac{4}{11}$ **[1]**

   (c) $\dfrac{9}{11}$ **[1]**

   (d) 0 **[1]**
2. **(a)** $1 - (0.1 + 0.2 + 0.25 + 0.1 + 0.15)$ **[1]** $= 0.2$ **[1]**

   (b) 0.15×60 **[1]** $= 9$ **[1]**
3. **(a)** HH, HT, TH, TT **[1]** $\dfrac{1}{4}$ **[1]**

   (b) HH, HT, TH, TT **[1]** $\dfrac{3}{4}$ **[1]**

4. **(a)** (D, T), (D, C), (D, H), (D, S), (N, T), (N, C), (N, H), (N, S), (P, T), (P, C), (P, H), (P, S) **[2]** **[1 if one missing or any repeated]**

   (b) 1 or 12 identified **[1]** $\dfrac{1}{12}$ **[1]**
5. **(a)**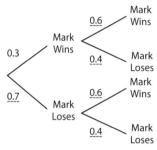

   0.7 **[1]**   0.6, 0.4, 0.6, 0.4 **[1]**

   (b) 0.3×0.6 **[1]** $= 0.18$ **[1]**

   (c) $1 - (0.7 \times 0.4) = 1 - 0.28$ **[1]** $= 0.72$ **[1]**
6.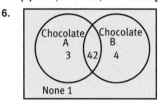

   (a) Fully correct with labels **[2]** **[1 for two numbers in the correct place]**

   (b) 1 identified **[1]** $\dfrac{1}{50}$ **[1]**

   (c) $\dfrac{3}{50}$ **[1]**

Statistics

1. Any suitable answer, e.g.

Horror	● ● ● ● ●
Romance	● ● ● ● ● ● ● ● ◖
Sci-Fi	● ● ● ● ● ● ● ◖
Thrillers	● ● ● ●

   Key: ● represents 2 people

   Suitable key **[1]**. Correctly completed pictogram for all four categories **[2]**.
2. Selecting a dual bar chart, vertical line graph or time series **[1]**

   Fully labelled **[1]**. Accurate bars/lines on chart **[1]**.
3. **(a)** Correct midpoints (12.5, 20, 30, 40, 50, 60, 70) **[1]**

   Total of 8150 **[1]**

   $8150 \div 200$ **[1]**

   Estimated mean = 40.8 kg (3 s.f.) **[1]**

   (b) Median interval $= 35 \leqslant w < 45$ **[1]**

   (c) Modal group $= 45 \leqslant w < 55$ **[1]**
4. 3, 3, 5, 6, 13. So greatest range = 10 **[3]**

GCSE Success

Maths

Foundation Tier

Exam Practice Workbook

Deborah Dobson,
Phil Duxbury,
Mike Fawcett and
Aftab Ilahi

Number

Algebra

Ratio, Proportion and Rates of Change

Contents

Geometry and Measures

Probability

Statistics

Practice Exam

1 **(a)** Work out −4 + −3 📱 [1 mark]

....

(b) Work out (−3 × −2) + (−5 × −3) 📱 [1 mark]

....

(c) Work out (−8 − −5) × (7 − 12) ÷ (−2 − 3) 📱 [1 mark]

....

2 Are the following **true** or **false**?

(a) −3 + −2 < −2 − +3 .... [1 mark]

(b) −5 − −7 = 11 + −9 .... [1 mark]

(c) −4 × −7 × −10 = 10 × −4 × 7 .... [1 mark]

(d) 26 ÷ 15 > −28 ÷ −15 .... [1 mark]

3 The temperature in New York is 8°C. It is 11°C colder in London.

(a) What is the temperature in London? [1 mark]

....

Moscow is three times colder than London.

(b) Work out the temperature in Moscow. [1 mark]

....

4 Given that 129 × 42 = 5418, calculate the following. 📱

(a) 1.29 × 4.2 .... [1 mark]

(b) 12.9 × 420 .... [1 mark]

(c) 5418 ÷ 0.42 .... [1 mark]

(d) 54.18 ÷ 0.129 .... [1 mark]

5 Bethany has £40. Tomorrow she will be paid £150 but will pay £225 for a holiday.

(a) How much debt will Bethany be in? [1 mark]

....

Bethany's father gives her $\frac{2}{5}$ of the amount she is in debt.

(b) How much debt is Bethany in now? [2 marks]

....

Score **/16**

For more help on this topic, see Letts GCSE Maths Foundation Revision Guide pages 4–5.

1 Write down all the factors of 48 which are:

(a) odd numbers [1 mark]

....

(b) square numbers [1 mark]

....

(c) multiples of 6 [1 mark]

....

2 James is thinking of a number between 1 and 50. It is 4 more than a prime number and 4 less than a square number. It is also a multiple of 3.

What could James's number be? [2 marks]

.... or ....

3 (a) Find the lowest common multiple (LCM) of 5 and 11. [1 mark]

....

(b) Find the highest common factor (HCF) of 14 and 35. [1 mark]

....

4 (a) Write 72 as a product of its prime factors. Give your answer in index form. [3 marks]

....

(b) Write 90 as a product of its prime factors. Give your answer in index form. [3 marks]

....

(c) Find the highest common factor (HCF) of 72 and 90. [2 marks]

....

(d) Find the lowest common multiple (LCM) of 72 and 90. [2 marks]

....

5 Bus A leaves the bus station every 12 minutes.
Bus B leaves the bus station every 28 minutes.
Bus A and Bus B both leave the bus station at 8.00am.

When will they next both leave the bus station at the same time? [3 marks]

....

Score   /20

For more help on this topic, see Letts GCSE Maths Foundation Revision Guide pages 6–7.

1 **(a)** Work out $5 + 2^2 \times 3$ 🖩 [1 mark]

....

(b) Work out $\frac{1}{5} + \frac{2}{5}$ 🖩 [1 mark]

....

(c) Write down the reciprocal of 4. 🖩 [1 mark]

....

2 Work out $\dfrac{(12 - 5 \times 2)^2}{5 - 3}$ .... [2 marks]

3 Calculate the following. Give your answers in their simplest form. 🖩

(a) $\frac{4}{5} \times \frac{3}{8}$ .... [2 marks]

(b) $\frac{5}{6} \div \frac{3}{10}$ .... [2 marks]

(c) $\frac{3}{4} - \frac{3}{5}$ .... [2 marks]

(d) $\frac{3}{5} + \frac{1}{3}$ .... [2 marks]

4 Wes is drawing storyboards for a new film. One day he completes $\frac{2}{5}$ of the drawings.

On the next day he completes $\frac{3}{7}$ of the drawings.

What fraction of the drawings has he got left to complete? 🖩 [3 marks]

....

5 A wall measures $1\frac{1}{4}$ m by $2\frac{2}{3}$ m.

Find the area of the wall, giving your answer as a mixed number. 🖩 [3 marks]

.... m²

6 Tank A and Tank B are identical water tanks.

Tank A is $\frac{3}{5}$ full. Tank B is $\frac{2}{9}$ full.

Tank B is emptied into Tank A.

What fraction of Tank A is now empty? 🖩 [3 marks]

....

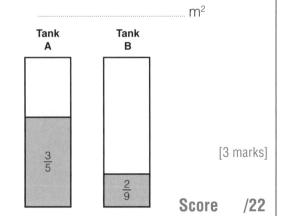

Score /22

For more help on this topic, see Letts GCSE Maths Foundation Revision Guide pages 8–9.

Operations

Module 3

1 Write the following in index form.

(a) $3 \times 3 \times 3 \times 3 \times 3 \times 3$ .... [1 mark]

(b) $12 \times 12 \times 12 \times 12$ .... [1 mark]

2 Write the following in order of value, smallest first.

2^5 $\sqrt[3]{64}$ 3^3 5^2 $\sqrt[4]{625}$ [1 mark]

....

3 Find the value of x in each of the following.

(a) $2^x = 128$ .... [1 mark]

(b) $\sqrt[3]{x} = 5$ .... [1 mark]

(c) $x^4 = 81$ .... [1 mark]

4 **(a)** Write $4^6 \div 4^4$ as a single power of 4. 🖩 .... [1 mark]

....

(b) Write $5^3 \times 5^{-5}$ as a single power of 5. 🖩 .... [1 mark]

....

(c) Write 3×10^{-4} as an ordinary number. 🖩 .... [1 mark]

....

5 **(a)** Write the following numbers in standard form. 🖩

    (i) 321 000 .... [1 mark]

    (ii) 0.000 605 .... [1 mark]

(b) Calculate the following. Leave your answer in standard form. 🖩

    (i) $(5 \times 10^3) \times (6 \times 10^{-8})$

.... [2 marks]

    (ii) $(4.1 \times 10^4) + (3.4 \times 10^3)$

.... [2 marks]

6 Work out the value of the following. 🖩

(a) 12^0 .... [1 mark]

(b) 4^{-2} .... [1 mark]

Soorc   /17

For more help on this topic, see Letts GCSE Maths Foundation Revision Guide pages 10–11.

Powers and Roots

Module 4

1 Write the following fractions as decimals. 🖩

(a) $\frac{7}{10}$ .... [1 mark]

(b) $\frac{15}{20}$ .... [1 mark]

(c) $\frac{9}{25}$ .... [1 mark]

2 Write the following in order of value, smallest first.

$\frac{12}{25}$ $\frac{3}{8}$ 0.475 $\frac{17}{51}$ [1 mark]

....

3 Write 56% as a fraction in its simplest form. 🖩   [1 mark]

....

4 Which of the fractions $\frac{5}{8}$ and $\frac{7}{11}$ is closest to $\frac{2}{3}$? Show your working. 🖩   [3 marks]

....

....

....

5 Calculate the following. 🖩

(a) 3.7×4.9 [2 marks]

....

(b) $56 \div 1.4$ [2 marks]

....

6 Carl orders 34 Creamy Crisp Doughnuts for a church event.

Each doughnut costs £1.29

Find the total cost of the doughnuts. Show your working. 🖩   [3 marks]

....

....

....

7 Find the decimal which is equivalent to $\frac{2}{9}$. 🖩   [1 mark]

....

Score   /16

For more help on this topic, see Letts GCSE Maths Foundation Revision Guide pages 12–13.

1 Round the following numbers to the degree of accuracy shown.

    (a) 3549 to the nearest hundred   [1 mark]

    (b) 28.54 to the nearest whole number   [1 mark]

    (c) 699 to the nearest ten   [1 mark]

2 Calculate the value of these numbers to the degree of accuracy shown.

    (a) $\sqrt{90}$ (2 decimal places)   [1 mark]

    (b) 2.56^2 (3 decimal places)   [1 mark]

    (c) $\sqrt[3]{175.6}$ (2 decimal places)   [1 mark]

3 **(a)** Round 404 928 to 2 significant figures.   [1 mark]

    (b) Round 0.04965 to 3 significant figures.   [1 mark]

    (c) Round π to 4 significant figures.   [1 mark]

4 Estimate $\dfrac{23 \times 2.8}{0.5}$ [2 marks]

5 Violet runs a coffee lounge. She wants to make 34 cups of coffee from a 500g bag of coffee.

    How much coffee should she use for each cup? Give your answer to 3 significant figures.

                                                      g   [2 marks]

6 Rachel works in a school office. She sends, on average, 72 letters home each week. Each letter costs 59p to send. There are 39 weeks in the school year.

    Estimate the cost of sending the letters home for the whole year.   [3 marks]

                             £

7 Ethan is 1.7m tall to 1 decimal place.

    Write down the limits of accuracy for his height.   [2 marks]

Score   /18

For more help on this topic, see Letts GCSE Maths Foundation Revision Guide pages 14–15.

Approximations

Module 6

1 Calculate the following. Write down all the figures on your calculator display.

(a) 4.5^4 .... [1 mark]

(b) $\sqrt[4]{2401}$ .... [1 mark]

(c) $\sqrt[7]{78125}$ .... [1 mark]

2 Calculate the following. Write down all the figures on your calculator display.

(a) $\dfrac{4+3.9^2}{5.2\times6.3}$ [2 marks]

(b) $\sqrt{4+3.1\times8}$ [2 marks]

3 **(a)** Work out $(3.5\times10^4)\times(4.9\times10^3)$ giving your answer in standard form. [1 mark]

....

(b) Work out $(4.56\times10^{-2})\div(3.8\times10^{-7})$ giving your answer in standard form. [1 mark]

....

4 Calculate the following using the fraction button on your calculator.

Give your answer as a mixed number.

(a) $14\frac{2}{3}-11\frac{5}{7}$ .... [1 mark]

(b) $4\frac{3}{10}\times7\frac{2}{9}$ .... [1 mark]

5 The Sun is 400 times further away from the Earth than the Moon.

The Sun is 1.496×10^8 km away from the Earth.

(a) How far away is the Moon from the Earth? Write your answer in standard form. [3 marks]

.... km

The Moon has a diameter of 3.48×10^3 km.

The Sun has a diameter of 1.392×10^6 km.

(b) How many times bigger is the Sun's diameter compared with the Moon's diameter? Write your answer in standard form. [3 marks]

....

Score /17

For more help on this topic, see Letts GCSE Maths Foundation Revision Guide pages 16–17.

10 **Module 7** **Answers Using Technology**

1 Simplify the following expressions. 📝

(a) $8a + 2 - 3a$ .... [1 mark]

(b) $6h + 3k + 9h - k$ .... [1 mark]

(c) $5a + 2b + 3c - 4a - 3a - 3c$ .... [1 mark]

(d) $3x^2 - 2x + 5x^2 + x + 1$ .... [1 mark]

2 Simplify the following expressions. 📝

(a) $3p^2 \times 2p^5$ .... [1 mark]

(b) $\left(3p^4\right)^3$ .... [1 mark]

(c) $18f^7g^2 \div 3f^2g$ .... [1 mark]

(d) $\left(2p^2\right)^{-3}$ .... [1 mark]

3 Simplify the following expressions where possible. 📝

(a) $60k^2 \div 5$ .... [1 mark]

(b) $\sqrt[4]{a^{12}}$ .... [1 mark]

(c) $\sqrt[3]{p^6} \times \sqrt[6]{p^3}$ .... [1 mark]

(d) $p^2 \times p^3 \times \sqrt{p^3}$ .... [1 mark]

4 Evaluate: 📝

(a) 4^{-1} .... [1 mark]

(b) $\left(\dfrac{2}{5}\right)^{-2}$ .... [1 mark]

(c) $32^{\frac{2}{5}}$ .... [1 mark]

(d) 16^0 .... [1 mark]

5 Which of the following are **equations** and which are **identities**? 📝

(a) $3x - 4 = (3x + 1) - (x - 5)$ .... [1 mark]

(b) $\dfrac{p+q}{pq} = \dfrac{1}{p} + \dfrac{1}{q}$ .... [1 mark]

(c) $x^2 + x^2 = 2x^2$ .... [1 mark]

(d) $x^2 + x^2 = x^4$ .... [1 mark]

(e) $\sqrt{a+b} = \sqrt{a} + \sqrt{b}$ .... [1 mark]

Score   /21

For more help on this topic, see Letts GCSE Maths Foundation Revision Guide pages 20–21.

1 Simplify:

(a) $6(a - 2)$ [2 marks]

(b) $3m(m + 2)$ [2 marks]

(c) $4n(2n - p)$ [2 marks]

(d) $5(d + 1) + 3(d - 1)$ [2 marks]

(e) $8(x + 2) - 2(2x - 3)$ [2 marks]

2 Multiply out the brackets:

(a) $(a + 3)(a + 2)$ [2 marks]

(b) $(f + 6)(f - 5)$ [2 marks]

(c) $(x - 5)(x - 7)$ [2 marks]

(d) $(a + 4)^2$ [2 marks]

(e) $(a - 9)^2$ [2 marks]

3 Factorise:

(a) $3a - 3b$ [2 marks]

(b) $6p + 8$ [2 marks]

(c) $x^2 - 7x$ [2 marks]

....

(d) $2pq - 6q$ [2 marks]

....

(e) $5p^2 - 10p$ [2 marks]

....

4 Write $3(2x-1)+4(x+8)+5$ in the form $a(bx+c)$ where a, b and c are integers. 🖩 [3 marks]

....

5 Factorise: 🖩

(a) $p^2 + 4p + 3$ [2 marks]

....

(b) $x^2 - 10x + 21$ [2 marks]

....

(c) $a^2 + 12a + 11$ [2 marks]

....

(d) $x^2 - x - 12$ [2 marks]

....

6 Factorise: 🖩

(a) $t^2 - 9$ [2 marks]

....

(b) $16 - f^2$ [2 marks]

....

(c) $1 - 25n^2$ [2 marks]

....

(d) $t^2 - 25$ [2 marks]

....

(e) $p^8 - 4$ [2 marks]

....

Score   /51

For more help on this topic, see Letts GCSE Maths Foundation Revision Guide pages 22–23.

1 If $x = 4$, $y = -2$ and $z = 3$, find the values of:

(a) $(x - y)^2$ [1 mark]

....

(b) $\dfrac{x^2}{y}$ [1 mark]

....

(c) $2z - y$ [1 mark]

....

(d) $xy + z$ [1 mark]

....

(e) $\sqrt{10x + 2y}$ [1 mark]

....

2 Rearrange $v = u + at$ to make a the subject. [2 marks]

....

3 Rearrange $y = \dfrac{2 + x}{5}$ to make x the subject. [2 marks]

....

4 Rearrange $y = \dfrac{2 + 3x}{x - 8}$ to make x the subject. [3 marks]

....

5 A briefcase weighs p grams when empty. When it is full of q grams of paper, it weighs r grams. Write down an equation for q in terms of p and r. [2 marks]

....

6 The formula to convert degrees Fahrenheit to degrees Celsius is $T_C = \dfrac{5(T_F - 32)}{9}$

(a) Use this formula to convert 88 degrees Fahrenheit (T_F) to degrees Celsius. [1 mark]

....

(b) Rearrange this formula to make T_F the subject. [2 marks]

....

(c) Now convert 60 degrees Celsius to degrees Fahrenheit. [1 mark]

....

Score /18

For more help on this topic, see Letts GCSE Maths Foundation Revision Guide pages 24–25.

1 Solve the equation $4x - 7 = 29$

[2 marks]

....

2 Solve the equation $5(x - 2) - 3(x - 4) = 4$ 🖩

[2 marks]

....

3 Solve the equation $\dfrac{x + 4}{5} = \dfrac{x - 2}{3}$

[3 marks]

....

4 Solve the equation $x^2 + 13x + 36 = 0$

[3 marks]

....

5 Solve, by factorisation, the equation $x^2 - 3x - 28 = 0$ 🖩

[3 marks]

....

6 $4x - 3y = 14$ and $x + y = 7$, find the values of x and y. 🖩

[4 marks]

$x =$ .... $y =$ ....

7 $4x + 2y = 10$ and $3x + 4y = 10$, find the values of x and y. 🖩

[4 marks]

$x =$ .... $y =$ ....

8 The diagram shows the graph of $y = x^2 - 7x + 4$

(a) By using the graph, solve (approximately) the equation $x^2 - 7x + 4 = 0$

[2 marks]

....

....

(b) By using the graph, solve (approximately) the equation $x^2 - 7x - 4 = 0$

[2 marks]

....

....

Score /25

For more help on this topic, see Letts GCSE Maths Foundation Revision Guide pages 26–27.

Algebraic Equations

Module 11

1 Solve the inequality $7x - 2 > 33$ 🖩 [2 marks]

....

2 Solve the inequality $5 - 2x \geqslant x + 8$ [2 marks]

....

3 Solve the inequality $58 > 20 - 2x$ [3 marks]

....

4 State the inequalities as shown on the number lines below. 🖩

(a) ....[1 mark]

(b) ....[1 mark]

(c) ....[1 mark]

5 List all integers x for which $-2 < x < 5$ 🖩 [2 marks]

....

6 List all integers x for which $-8 < x \leqslant -4$ 🖩 [2 marks]

....

7 List all integers x for which $3 \leqslant 2x \leqslant 13$ 🖩 [2 marks]

....

8 Solve the inequality $5 - 2x < 8x$, showing your solution on a number line. 🖩 [3 marks]

....

9 Find the integer value(s) of x for which $2x - 3 > 5$ and $12 - x > 6$ 🖩 [5 marks]

....

10 List all integers x for which $-2 < 10 - x < 7$ 🖩 [2 marks]

....

Score   /26

For more help on this topic, see Letts GCSE Maths Foundation Revision Guide pages 28–29.

1 Here are the first four terms of an arithmetic sequence:

8   12   16   20

Write down the next two terms in the sequence. 🖩   [2 marks]

....

2 Here are the first four terms of an arithmetic sequence:

41   32   23   14

Write down the next two terms in the sequence. 🖩   [2 marks]

....

3 A term-to-term sequence is given by $U_{n+1} = 5U_n - 2$ where $U_1 = 1$

Write down the first five terms in this sequence. 🖩   [2 marks]

....

4 An arithmetic sequence has the formula $U_n = 9n - 1$.

Write down the first four terms in this sequence. 🖩   [2 marks]

....

5 11, 15, 19, 23, … are the first four terms in an arithmetic sequence. 🖩

(a) Find an expression for U_n, the position-to-term formula.   [2 marks]

....

(b) Is 303 a number in this sequence? Explain your answer.   [2 marks]

....

6 Here are the first four terms of an arithmetic sequence:

15   17   19   21

(a) The sequence may be expressed by using a term-to-term formula
$U_{n+1} = U_n + d$ with $U_1 = a$. Write down the values of a and d.   [2 marks]

$a =$ .... $d =$ ....

(b) Find an expression for U_n, the position-to-term formula.   [2 marks]

....

7 The position-to-term formula of a geometric sequence is given by $U_n = \left(\dfrac{1}{3}\right)^n$.
Write down the first four terms in this sequence.   [4 marks]

....

Score   /20

For more help on this topic, see Letts GCSE Maths Foundation Revision Guide pages 30–31.

Sequences

Module 13

1 Find the gradients of the following lines labelled A, B, C and D. 🖉 [4 marks]

A: $y = 6x - 7$ B: $y = 8 - 3x$

C: $2x + 3y + 4 = 0$ D: $y - x = 0$

Line A: Gradient is .... Line C: Gradient is ....

Line B: Gradient is .... Line D: Gradient is ....

2 From the following lines, write down the two that are parallel. 🖉 [2 marks]

A: $3y = x - 6$ B: $4x + 2y = 8$

C: $x = 3y - 12$ D: $2y - x + 2 = 0$

Lines .... and .... are parallel.

3 Write down the equation of the y-axis. [1 mark]

....

4 A line has gradient -6 and passes through the point (0, 9).

Find the equation of the line. [2 marks]

....

5 Work out the equation of the line parallel to $y = 5x - 2$ that passes through the point (–3, 1). [3 marks]

....

6 A parallelogram has one vertex in each of the four quadrants. Three of the vertices have coordinates (1, 3), (2, −1) and (−3, 1).

By drawing a diagram, find the coordinates of the fourth vertex. [3 marks]

....

7 Find the equation of the line joining points (–4, –10) and (6, –5). [4 marks]

Score /19

For more help on this topic, see Letts GCSE Maths Foundation Revision Guide pages 32–33.

1 This is the graph of the quadratic curve $y = x^2 + 2x - 15$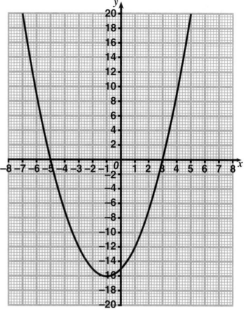

Using the graph:

(a) Write down the roots of the
equation $x^2 + 2x - 15 = 0$ [2 marks]

$x = $ .... and

$x = $ ....

(b) Write down the coordinates of
the intercept with the y-axis.   [1 mark]

....

(c) Write down the coordinates of
the turning point on the graph.   [2 marks]

....

2 Find (using algebra) the roots of the equation $x^2 - 7x - 44 = 0$ [3 marks]

....

3 This is the graph of $y = 5 + 2x - x^2$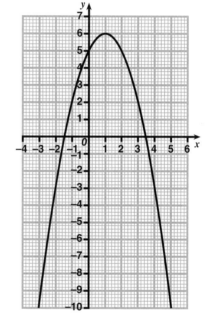

Using the graph:

(a) Write down the roots of the equation
$5 + 2x - x^2 = 0$ [2 marks]

$x = $ .... and $x = $ ....

(b) Write down the coordinates of the
intercept with the y-axis.   [1 mark]

....

(c) Write down the equation of the line of
symmetry of the graph.   [2 marks]

....

4 Consider the curve $y = x^2 - 8x + 3$. Without drawing the graph:

(a) Write down the equation of the line of symmetry of the curve.   [2 marks]

....

(b) Work out the coordinates of the minimum point on the curve.   [2 marks]

....

Score   /17

For more help on this topic, see Letts GCSE Maths Foundation Revision Guide pages 34–35.

Module 15

1 For the function $f(x) = 12x + 5$, write down the outputs for each of the following inputs:

Input x		Output $f(x)$
0	→	....
1	→	....
2	→	.... [3 marks]

2 Find the function given by the following mapping:

Input x		Output $f(x)$
2	→	3
3	→	6
4	→	9 [2 marks]

....

3 For the function $f(x) = \dfrac{x+3}{2}$, write down the inputs for each of the following outputs:

Input x		Output $f(x)$
....	→	4
....	→	4.5
....	→	5 [3 marks]

4 **(a)** On the grid, sketch graphs of: 📱

    (i) $y = x^3$ [2 marks]

    (ii) $y = \dfrac{1}{x}$ [2 marks]

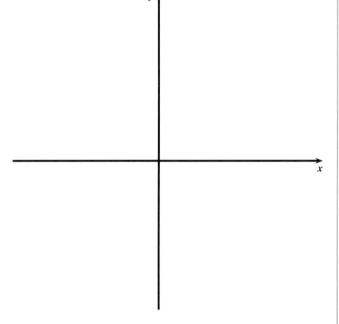

(b) Write down the number of solutions there are to the equation $x^3 = \dfrac{1}{x}$
(you do not have to find the solutions).   [1 mark]

....

5 Four different graphs are illustrated below. Match the correct line with its graph.

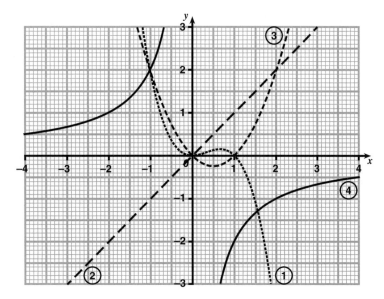

Choose from: $y = -\dfrac{2}{x}$, $y = x$, $y = x^2 - x^3$, $y = x^2 - x$ [4 marks]

Line 1 ....

Line 2 ....

Line 3 ....

Line 4 ....

6 Sketch the graphs of $y = \dfrac{2}{x}$ and $y = \dfrac{-4}{x}$ on the same axes. 🔲 [4 marks]

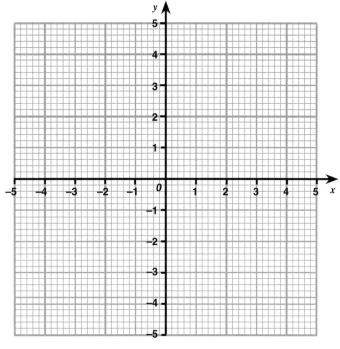

Score /21

For more help on this topic, see Letts GCSE Maths Foundation Revision Guide pages 36–37.

Module 16

1 The following shows a distance–time graph for Max walking to college and back.

(a) If Max set off at 9.30am, what time did he reach college? [1 mark]

....

(b) For how long did Max stay at college? [1 mark]

....

(c) What was Max's speed on his way home? [2 marks]

....

2 The following shows a speed–time graph for a train.

(a) Calculate the initial acceleration of the train. [2 marks]

....

(b) For how long was the train travelling with constant speed? [1 mark]

....

(c) How far did the train travel in the first 15 seconds? [2 marks]

....

3 The following graph is used by a taxi firm to calculate the cost of a single journey.

(a) How much is the standing charge? [1 mark]

....

(b) How much does a journey of six miles cost? [1 mark]

....

(c) Work out the cost per mile that the taxi firm charges, not including the standing charge. [2 marks]

....

Score   /13

For more help on this topic, see Letts GCSE Maths Foundation Revision Guide pages 38–39.

1 Calculate the area of a rectangle with width 850mm and length 1.25m. [2 marks]

....

2 Convert 3.4km² to metres². 🖩 [2 marks]

....

3 If 1cm³ of water has a mass of 1g, what is the mass of 1m³ of water in kilograms? 🖩 [2 marks]

....

4 5 miles = 8km

Which is faster, 68mph or 110km/h? [2 marks]

....

5 Convert 24m/s to kilometres per hour. [3 marks]

....

6 Shahida works 30 hours each week and earns £18.40/h.

Bob works 35 hours each week and earns £626.00.

Leila works 32 hours each week and earns £30 000 per annum.

(a) Who has the best hourly rate? [3 marks]

....

(b) Who earns the most per year? [2 marks]

....

7 Here are two pieces of gold:

Block A has a volume of 24cm³ and a mass of 463g.

The volume of block B is 30cm³ and it contains exactly the same quality of gold.

A   B

(a) Calculate the density of the gold. [2 marks]

....

(b) Calculate the mass of block B. [2 marks]

....

(c) If the price of gold is £23.50/g, calculate the total value of both pieces. [2 marks]

....

Score   /22

Converting Measurements

Module 18

For more help on this topic, see Letts GCSE Maths Foundation Revision Guide pages 42–43.

1 A model plane is made using a scale of 1 : 20

(a) If the wingspan of the model is 3m, what is the wingspan of the actual plane? [1 mark]

....

(b) If the plane is 57m long, how long is the model? [2 marks]

....

2 Here is a map with a scale of 1 : 5 000 000

(a) What is the distance on the map between Bristol and Leeds? [1 mark]

....

(b) What is the actual distance? [2 marks]

....

(c) Measure the bearing of Exeter from Leeds. .... [2 marks]

(d) What is the bearing of Leeds from Exeter? .... [2 marks]

3 A cruise ship sets off from harbour A for 100km on a bearing of 075° to point B.
It then changes to a bearing of 220° and sails at 15km/h for 6 hours to point C.
Finally it heads straight back to the harbour (A).

(a) Draw an accurate diagram to show the journey using a scale of 1cm:20km   [2 marks]

(b) Measure the bearing and distance of the last leg of the journey from C to A.   [2 marks]

Bearing: ....   Distance: .... km

4 A map is drawn to a scale of 1:25 000

Villages S and R are 18cm apart on the map.

(a) Work out the actual distance between S and R in kilometres.   [2 marks]

....

R is due West of S. T is another village. The bearing of T from R is 040° and
the bearing of T from S is 320°.

(b) Draw a diagram to show the positions of S, R and T.   [2 marks]

Score   /18

For more help on this topic, see Letts GCSE Maths Foundation Revision Guide pages 44–45.

Scales, Diagrams and Maps

Module 19

1 Circle the numbers which are **not** equivalent to 3.75 ▣ [2 marks]

$\dfrac{30}{8}$ 37.5%   375% $\dfrac{14}{5}$ $3\dfrac{5}{8}$ $\dfrac{750}{200}$

2 Write the following numbers in ascending order. ▣ [2 marks]

0.21   20% $\dfrac{3}{10}$ 0.211 $\dfrac{2}{9}$

3 Is 2.125 or $2\dfrac{4}{5}$ closer to $2\dfrac{1}{2}$? Explain your reasoning. ▣ [2 marks]

4 On a new estate of 32 houses, $\dfrac{3}{8}$ have two bedrooms. $\dfrac{5}{6}$ of the two-bedroom houses have a garage.

What percentage of the whole estate is represented by two-bedroom houses with a garage? [2 marks]

5 Claire makes soft toys to sell at a Christmas market.

(a) Each dog toy costs £3.45 to make and Claire sells them for £5.99.

What is her percentage profit? [2 marks]

(b) A tiger toy costs 15% more to make than a dog toy and she makes 80 tiger toys. Claire sells 55 of them for £6.99 and the rest at the reduced price of £4.

What percentage profit does she make on tiger toys? [4 marks]

6 At Mathstown School 55% of the students are girls. 40% of the girls and 65% of the boys have school lunch.

(a) What percentage of students at the school have school lunch? [3 marks]

(b) What fraction of the boys do not have school lunch? [2 marks]

Score   /19

For more help on this topic, see Letts GCSE Maths Foundation Revision Guide pages 46–47.

1 Simplify these ratios and circle the odd one out. You must show all your working. 🖩 [2 marks]

£4 : £6   10 : 15   20cm : 3m   750g : 1.125kg   40 seconds : 1 minute

....

....

....

2 Jane is making 'mist blue' paint for her room. She mixes navy blue, grey and white paint in the ratio 1 : 2 : 7

  (a) How much of each colour does Jane need to make 2 litres of 'mist blue' paint?   [3 marks]

  Navy blue: .... ml   Grey: .... ml   White: .... ml

  (b) Jane finds she has $\frac{3}{4}$ litres of navy blue, 1200ml of grey and 6 litres of white paint.

  What is the maximum amount of 'mist blue' she can make?   [2 marks]

  .... litres

3 The ratio of A : B is 5 : 8

  Complete this statement. A is $\frac{\Box}{\Box}$ of B. 🖩   [1 mark]

4 This is a recipe for shortbread:

Makes 15 biscuits			
110g butter	50g sugar	175g flour	50g chocolate chips

  (a) Amil has 70g of sugar. How many biscuits can he make?   [2 marks]

  ....

  (b) How much flour is needed to make 12 biscuits?   [2 marks]

  .... g

5 Lucy makes green paint by mixing yellow and blue paint in the ratio 5 : 2
Blue paint costs £30 for 5 litres and yellow paint costs £28 for 7 litres.

  Lucy sells her green paint for £4.50 per litre. Will she make a profit? Show your working to justify your decision. 🖩   [3 marks]

....

....

....

Score   /15

For more help on this topic, see Letts GCSE Maths Foundation Revision Guide pages 48–49.

Ratio

Module 21

1 If Shabir has 250ml of soup for her lunch, how many kilocalories of energy will she get?

.... [2 marks]

2 Leon changes £500 to euros at the rate shown and goes to France on holiday.

| £1 = 1.29 euros | £1 = 187.99 Japanese yen |
| £1 = 1.56 US dollars | £1 = 97.04 Indian rupees |

(a) How many euros does he take on holiday? .... [1 mark]

Leon spends €570.

(b) He changes his remaining euros on the ferry where the exchange rate is £1 : €1.33

How much in pounds sterling does he take home? .... [2 marks]

3 Fred's dairy herd of 80 cattle produces 1360 litres of milk per day.

(a) If Fred buys another 25 cattle and is paid 30p/litre, what will his annual milk income be? .... [4 marks]

(b) If 6 tonnes of hay will last 80 cattle for 10 days, how long will the same amount of hay last the increased herd? [2 marks]

....

4 Similar triangles are the same shape. Triangles *PQR* and *STU* are similar.

Find the missing lengths *PR* and *TU*. [4 marks]

PR = ...

TU = ...

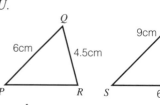

5 Two similar cylinders P and Q have surface areas of 120cm² and 270cm².

(a) Calculate the scale factor of their areas. [1 mark]

....

(b) What is the scale factor of the heights of the two cylinders? [2 marks]

....

(c) If the volume of Q is 2700cm³, what is the volume of P? [3 marks]

.... cm³

Score /21

For more help on this topic, see Letts GCSE Maths Foundation Revision Guide pages 50–51.

1 (a) Peter invests £10000 in a savings account which pays 2% compound interest per annum.

How much will his investment be worth after four years? [2 marks]

....

(b) Paul invests £10000 in company shares.
In the first year the shares increase in value by 15%.
In the second year they increase by 6%.
In the third year they lose 18% of their value.
In the fourth year the shares increase by 1%.

What is his investment worth after four years? .... [3 marks]

2 Lazya invests £6500 at 3% compound interest for three years. She works out the first year's interest to be £195. She tells her family she will earn £585 over three years.

Is she right? Show working to justify your decision. [3 marks]

....

....

3 This graph shows a tank being filled with water and then emptied. 📝

(a) How deep is the water when the tank is full?

.... [1 mark]

(b) Between what times is the tank filling fastest?

.... [1 mark]

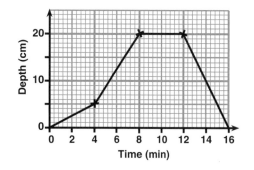

(c) Work out the rate of decrease of water level as the tank empties. .... [1 mark]

4 This graph shows the distance travelled by a cyclist for the first 10 seconds of a race.

(a) What distance does the cyclist travel in the first 8 seconds? [2 marks]

....

(b) Work out the cyclist's average speed for the first 10 seconds. [2 marks]

....

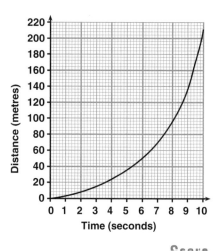

Score   /15

For more help on this topic, see Letts GCSE Maths Foundation Revision Guide pages 52–53.

1 Using only a ruler and a pair of compasses, construct a triangle with sides 8cm, 7cm and 9cm.

[2 marks]

2 Using only a ruler and a pair of compasses, construct a rectangle with one side 8cm and an area of 28cm^2.

[2 marks]

3 Using only a ruler and a pair of compasses, draw a line PQ such that angle PQR is 90°.

[2 marks]

Q _____ R

4 This is a plan of a field using a scale of 1cm : 10m

The farmer wants to install a water trough. It must be:

- at least 15m from the tree
- more than 20m from the fence *DC*
- nearer to *AB* than to *AD*.

Shade the area where the farmer can put the trough. [3 marks]

5 Using only a ruler and a pair of compasses, construct an angle of 30°. [3 marks]

Score /12

For more help on this topic, see Letts GCSE Maths Foundation Revision Guide pages 56–57.

Constructions

Module 24

1 Will a regular pentagon tessellate? Use a diagram in your explanation. [2 marks]

....

....

....

....

2 The internal angles of a regular polygon are 135°.

How many sides has the polygon? [2 marks]

....

3 *ABIJKL* and *BCDEFGHI* are regular polygons. Calculate angle *JIH*. [3 marks]

....

4 Calculate angle *FED*. State all your reasons. [3 marks]

....

....

....

....

5 Lines *BC* and *DE* are parallel. Calculate angle *CPR*, giving all your reasons. [2 marks]

....

....

Score /12

For more help on this topic, see Letts GCSE Maths Foundation Revision Guide pages 58–59.

1 Draw lines to match each triangle with its correct description. [3 marks]

A   B   C   D   E

| Scalene | Right-angled isosceles | Equilateral | Obtuse scalene | Obtuse isosceles |

2 Use this diagram to prove the angle sum of a triangle is 180°. [3 marks]

P ———— B ————→ Q

b

a c

R A C S

....
....
....
....

3 Use this diagram to find the angle sum of an octagon. [3 marks]

....

4 Complete this sentence with the name of the correct quadrilateral.

A .... has two pairs of equal sides but only one pair of equal angles. [1 mark]

5 Find angle x, giving all your reasons. [3 marks]

x

....
....
....
....

Score   /13

For more help on this topic, see Letts GCSE Maths Foundation Revision Guide pages 60–61.

1 Circle the two similar triangles. [1 mark]

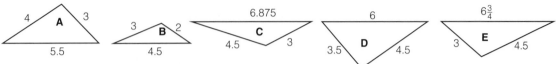

2 Circle the two congruent triangles. [1 mark]

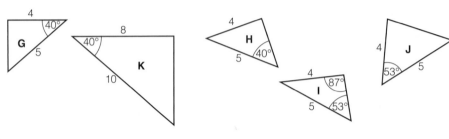

3 Triangle *FGH* and triangle *PQR* are similar.

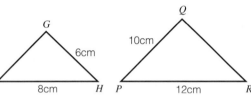

Calculate:

(a) *QR* [2 marks]

....

(b) *FG* [2 marks]

....

4 State whether these triangles are congruent and give your reasons. [2 marks]

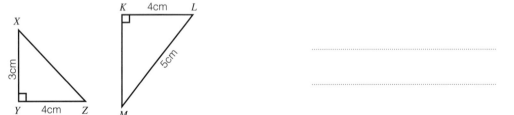

....

....

....

5 The dimensions of a £10 note are 142mm × 75mm and those of a £50 note are 156mm × 85mm.

Are the two notes mathematically similar? Explain your reasoning. [3 marks]

....

....

....

Score /11

For more help on this topic, see Letts GCSE Maths Foundation Revision Guide pages 62–63.

1 (a) Describe the transformation
that moves A on to B. [2 marks]

....

....

(b) Describe the transformation that
moves B on to C. [2 marks]

....

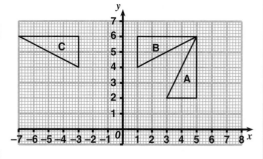

2 Describe fully the single transformation
that maps P on to Q. [3 marks]

....

....

....

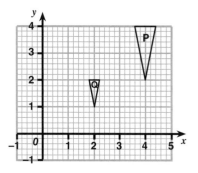

3 (a) Plot the triangle T with coordinates
(3, 3), (3, 1) and (4, 1). [1 mark]

(b) Rotate T 90° clockwise with centre
(0, 0) and label the image V. [2 marks]

(c) Reflect V in the *y*-axis and label the
image W. [2 marks]

(d) What transformation maps V back
on to T? [2 marks]

....

....

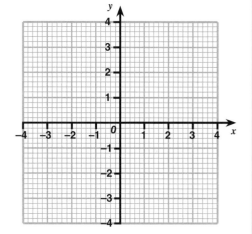

4 Enlarge this shape with:

(a) scale factor 2, centre (3, 5) [2 marks]

(b) scale factor 0.5, centre (0, 0) [2 marks]

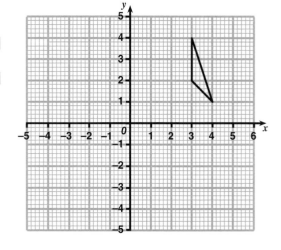

Score   /18

For more help on this topic, see Letts GCSE Maths Foundation Revision Guide pages 64–65.

Transformations

1 Complete the following statements with the correct word.

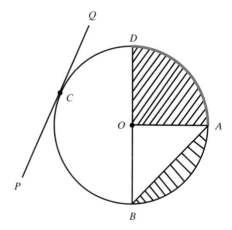

(a) *OA* is the _____ of the circle. [1 mark]

(b) *BD* is a _____ . [1 mark]

(c) *PCQ* is a _____ to the circle at *C*. [1 mark]

(d) The curved line around the full circle is the _____ . [1 mark]

(e) The blue line *AD* is an _____ . [1 mark]

(f) The shaded area *OAD* is a _____ . [1 mark]

(g) The shaded area between *A* and *B* is a _____ . [1 mark]

(h) *OAB* is an _____ triangle. [1 mark]

2 Calculate the circumference of this circle. Give your answer to 2 significant figures. [3 marks]

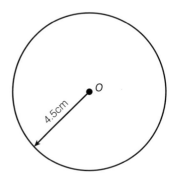

_____ cm

3 Calculate the area of a circle with diameter 8cm. Give your answer in terms of π. [3 marks]

....

4 What is the perimeter of this shape? [2 marks]

8cm

4cm

5cm

.... cm

5 This is the net for a cone.

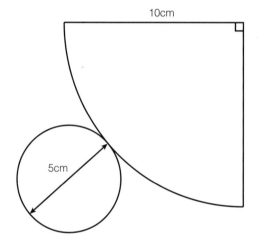

10cm

5cm

Calculate the surface area. [4 marks]

....

6 A plane circles the Earth at an altitude of 11km.

If the radius of the Earth is 6370km, how much further does the plane travel than someone making the same journey at sea-level? [3 marks]

.... km

Score   /23

For more help on this topic, see Letts GCSE Maths Foundation Revision Guide pages 66–67.

Circles

Module 29

1 What 3D shape has 6 faces, 10 edges and 6 vertices? [2 marks]

....

2 Sketch two different 3D solids with five faces and name them. [3 marks]

3 Draw the plan and elevations of this 3D shape. [4 marks]

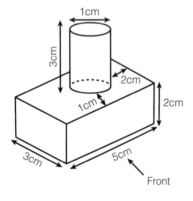

4 Sketch the 3D shape shown by this plan and elevations. [3 marks]

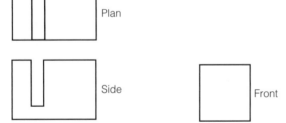

Score   /12

For more help on this topic, see Letts GCSE Maths Foundation Revision Guide pages 68–69.

1 Calculate the area and perimeter of these shapes.

(a)

[3 marks]

Area: .... m²

Perimeter: .... m

(b)

[3 marks]

Area: .... cm²

Perimeter: .... cm

2 Calculate the area of this shape.

[2 marks]

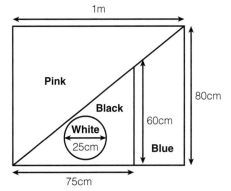

....

3 Look at this design for a flag.

[flag design with labels: 1m, Pink, Black, White, 25cm, 80cm, 60cm, Blue, 75cm]

Calculate the area of this flag that is:

(a) pink

[2 marks]

....

(b) blue

[2 marks]

....

(c) black

[2 marks]

....

4 Calculate the surface area of a cylinder with radius 4cm and height 5cm.
Give your answer in terms of π. [3 marks]

.... cm²

5 This shape is a cone of vertical height 4cm sitting on a cube of side 3cm.
Calculate its volume. [3 marks]

4cm

3cm

....

6 A sphere of radius 3.5cm and a cube with sides a cm have the same volume.

Find a. Give your answer to 3 significant figures. [3 marks]

.... cm

7 Calculate the volume of a hemisphere with radius 5cm.
Give your answer in terms of π. [3 marks]

....

8 Which has the larger surface area, a cuboid
with dimensions 4.4cm × 5.3cm × 1.8cm
or a hemisphere with radius 2.8cm? [4 marks]

....

Score /30

For more help on this topic, see Letts GCSE Maths Foundation Revision Guide pages 70–71.

1 (a) Work out the size of angle p.

[3 marks]

....

(b) Find the length KL. Give your answer to 3 significant figures.

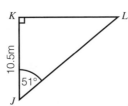

[3 marks]

.... m

2 (a) Calculate the length NP.

[2 marks]

....

(b) Find angle NOP.

[3 marks]

....

3 Find q, leaving your answer as a square root.

[3 marks]

....

4 (a) Write down the value of:

(i) sin 45°

.... [1 mark]

(ii) tan 45°

.... [1 mark]

(b) Calculate a and b.

[4 marks]

$a =$ ....

$b =$ ....

5 A builder uses a ramp to push his wheelbarrow on to a platform.

If the platform is 1m high and the ramp is 5m long, what angle does the ramp make with the ground?

[3 marks]

....

Score /23

For more help on this topic, see Letts GCSE Maths Foundation Revision Guide pages 72–73.

Module 32

1 Here are base vectors **r**, **s** and **t** drawn on isometric paper.

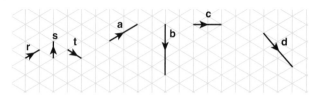

Write each of the vectors **a** to **d** in terms of **r**, **s** and **t**. [4 marks]

a = ... **b** = ... **c** = ... **d** = ...

2 *OPQRST* is a regular hexagon. *X* is the midpoint of *QR*.

$\overrightarrow{OP}$ = **a**, $\overrightarrow{OT}$ = **b** and $\overrightarrow{PQ}$ = **c**.

Write the following vectors in terms of **a**, **b** and **c**.

(a) $\overrightarrow{QR}$ .... [1 mark]

(b) $\overrightarrow{RQ}$ .... [1 mark]

(c) $\overrightarrow{OQ}$ .... [1 mark]

(d) $\overrightarrow{SQ}$ .... [1 mark]

(e) $\overrightarrow{QT}$ .... [1 mark]

(f) $\overrightarrow{TX}$ .... [1 mark]

3 *ABCD* is a parallelogram.
BE is a straight line with *AB* = *AE*.
$\overrightarrow{AB}$ = **b** and $\overrightarrow{AD}$ = **d**.

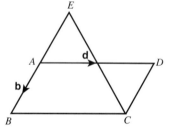

(a) Write $\overrightarrow{BE}$ in terms of **b** and **d**. .... [1 mark]

(b) Write $\overrightarrow{AC}$ in terms of **b** and **d**. .... [2 marks]

(c) Write $\overrightarrow{CE}$ in terms of **b** and **d**. .... [2 marks]

4 *PQR* is an equilateral triangle.
OPQ is an isosceles triangle with *OQ* = *PQ*
$\overrightarrow{OQ}$ = **q** and $\overrightarrow{OP}$ = **p**.

Find $\overrightarrow{OR}$, $\overrightarrow{PQ}$ and $\overrightarrow{PR}$. [3 marks]

$\overrightarrow{OR}$ = ... $\overrightarrow{PQ}$ = ... $\overrightarrow{PR}$ = ...

Score **/18**

For more help on this topic, see Letts GCSE Maths Foundation Revision Guide pages 74–75.

1 A fair dice is rolled. Mark on the probability scale the probability of rolling:

(a) an odd number, P(odd)   [1 mark]

(b) a 5 or a 6, P(5 or 6)   [1 mark]

(c) a 7, P(7)   [1 mark]

```
├──────┬──────┬──────┬──────┬──────┬──────┤
0             0.5                         1
```

2 There are three bananas, five oranges, four apples and two mangoes in a fruit bowl. A piece of fruit is taken at random.

Find the probability that it is:

(a) an apple   ....   [1 mark]

(b) a banana or a mango   ....   [1 mark]

(c) not an orange   ....   [1 mark]

3 The table shows the probability that Mark will choose a certain activity when he gets home from school on any given day.

Activity	Watch TV	Do homework	Play on computer	Go for a bike ride	Other
Probability	0.2		0.3	0.25	0.1

Find the probability that Mark will do homework on any given day.   [2 marks]

....

4 Brian bought a dice from the joke shop. He rolled it 25 times and recorded the results. Here are the results:

Number	1	2	3	4	5	6
Frequency	0	3	2	4	4	12

(a) Find the relative frequency of rolling a 6.   [1 mark]

....

Brian rolls the dice another 250 times.

(b) How many times would he be expected to get an even number?   [3 marks]

....

Score   /12

For more help on this topic, see Letts GCSE Maths Foundation Revision Guide pages 78–79.

1 A fair dice and a coin are thrown at the same time.

List all the possible outcomes. The first one is done for you. [2 marks]

(1, head) ....

....

2 A fair dice is thrown and a spinner is spun. The spinner has three equal sides – one side marked 1, a second side marked 3 and a third side marked 5. The scores on the dice and spinner are added together.

(a) Draw a sample space diagram to show all the possible outcomes. [2 marks]

(b) What is the probability of getting a score higher than 7? [1 mark]

....

(c) Find the probability of scoring an even number. [1 mark]

....

3 Fifty students are invited to vote for a new class president. They can each vote for a maximum of two people from Luke (L), Dan (D) and Jack (J).

Luke gets 26 votes altogether   Dan gets 17 votes altogether
7 students vote for Dan and Luke   4 students vote for Luke and Jack
2 students vote for Dan and Jack   3 students don't vote

(a) Complete the Venn diagram to show this information. The universal set ε contains all 50 students. [3 marks]

(b) Find the probability that a student chosen at random votes for Jack only. [1 mark]

....

Score /10

For more help on this topic, see Letts GCSE Maths Foundation Revision Guide pages 80–81.

1   A washing powder manufacturer conducts a survey of the actual weight of powder in the 500g boxes on the production line.

A sample of 12 boxes is taken over a period of 1 hour:

495, 503, 490, 505, 490, 498, 500, 510, 505, 498, 498, 501

(a) What is the mode for the sample?   [1 mark]

....

(b) Find the median.   [1 mark]

....

(c) The manufacturer produces 10 000 boxes per hour.
    Give two reasons why this may not be a good sample.   [2 marks]

....

....

2   The table shows the weights of 160 different species of birds in a forest.

Weight (g)	Frequency
$30 \leqslant w < 40$	20
$40 \leqslant w < 50$	25
$50 \leqslant w < 60$	22
$60 \leqslant w < 80$	44
$80 \leqslant w < 100$	32
$100 \leqslant w < 120$	15
$120 \leqslant w < 150$	2
	160

(a) Which class interval contains the median?   [1 mark]

....

(b) Calculate an estimate of the mean weight of the birds.   [3 marks]

....

(c) What percentage of the birds weigh less than 80g?   [2 marks]

....

3   There are five cards with an integer on each. The mean of all the numbers on the cards is 7. Both the mode and the median of the numbers are 6.

What numbers could be on the cards? 📝   [3 marks]

....

Score   /13

For more help on this topic, see Letts GCSE Maths Foundation Revision Guide pages 84–85.

1 The table shows the sales figures for a car dealership over two different weeks.

(a) There were 100 car sales in total in week 2.
Complete the table. [1 mark]

(b) Show this data in a suitable chart. [3 marks]

Sales	Week 1	Week 2
Monday	10	25
Tuesday	25	20
Wednesday	29	15
Thursday	40	19
Friday	16	

2 Sixty cat owners were asked about which treats they buy for their cats:

• 35 said they bought Biscuit Treats

• 19 said they bought Meaty Sticks

• 14 owners said they bought both products

Complete the Venn diagram. [3 marks]

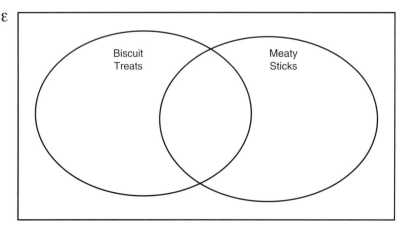

3 The manager of a pizza shop conducts a survey of favourite pizzas. She wants to show this information on a pie chart.

	Frequency	Angle
Vegetarian	45	60°
Seafood	80	
Meat	50	
Chicken	40	
Mushroom		

Complete the table. [2 marks]

4 The table shows the sales of a particular type of mobile phone over an eight-year period.

Year	1	2	3	4	5	6	7	8
Sales (millions)	2	10	20	40	70	125	150	170

(a) By plotting a suitable graph, use this information to predict the sales for year 9. [3 marks]

....

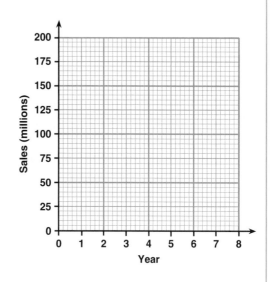

(b) Comment on the reliability of using your graph to predict sales in year 14. [2 marks]

....

....

5 The speeds of 12 drivers and their ages were recorded in the table below. John says that 'younger drivers drive too fast'.

Age (years)	20	32	24	30	22	40	35	34	42	22	38	32
Speed (mph)	38	30	37	32	39	30	32	33	28	36	27	34

(a) Use an appropriate diagram to comment on whether the data supports John's conclusion. [3 marks]

....

....

....

(b) Describe the relationship between age and driving speed. [1 mark]

....

....

Score   /18

For more help on this topic, see Letts GCSE Maths Foundation Revision Guide pages 86–87.

Module 37

1 Complete the table with a tick (✓) or a cross (✗). The first row has been completed for you. [2 marks]

	Represents a single value	Affected by outliers	Measure of spread
Mode	✓	✗	✗
Median			
Mean			
Range			

2 The test scores of 24 students in a history exam are given below.

Class A	33	45	67	83	56	23	57	45	73	43	26	35
Class B	33	27	40	44	78	28	49	38	54	32	51	74

Which class did better? Give reasons for your answer. [5 marks]

....

....

....

....

....

....

3 Claire surveys 40 members of her running club to find out how far they run every week.

She analyses her results and calculates the mean as 8.5 miles and the median as 7 miles. She then decides to include her own distance of 9 miles.

(a) The new mean is: [1 mark]

Lower ☐   No different ☐   Higher ☐

Reason: ....

....

(b) What will be the effect on the median once Claire's distance is included in the results? [1 mark]

....

....

4 The tables below show the results of a survey on the cost of car insurance for 30–50 year olds and for under 30 year olds.

30–50 year olds

Cost (£)	Frequency		
$100 \leqslant c < 150$	10		
$150 \leqslant c < 200$	38		
$200 \leqslant c < 250$	48		
$250 \leqslant c < 300$	31		
$300 \leqslant c < 350$	20		
$350 \leqslant c < 400$	8		
$400 \leqslant c < 500$	5		

Under 30s

Cost (£)	Frequency		
$100 \leqslant c < 150$	2		
$150 \leqslant c < 200$	15		
$200 \leqslant c < 250$	10		
$250 \leqslant c < 300$	21		
$300 \leqslant c < 350$	42		
$350 \leqslant c < 400$	45		
$400 \leqslant c < 500$	25		

Compare the cost of insurance for the two sets of drivers.   [5 marks]

Comparison 1: ....

....

....

Comparison 2: ....

....

....

Score   /14

For more help on this topic, see Letts GCSE Maths Foundation Revision Guide pages 88–89.

Comparing Distributions

Module 38

GCSE
Mathematics
Foundation tier

Paper 1   Time: 1 hour 30 minutes

| **For this paper you must have:** |
| • mathematical instruments |
| You must **not** use a calculator. |

Instructions

- Use black ink or black ball-point pen. Draw diagrams in pencil.
- Read each question carefully before you start to write your answer.
- Diagrams are not accurately drawn unless otherwise stated.
- Answer **all** the questions.
- Answer the questions in the space provided.
- In all calculations, show clearly how you work out your answer. Use a separate sheet of paper if needed. Marks may be given for a correct method even if the answer is wrong.

Information

- The mark for each question is shown in brackets.
- The maximum mark for this paper is 80.

Name: ....

1. **(a)** Work out

    $20 + 3 \times 2$ [1]

    ....

    (b) Write 30% as a decimal.   [1]

    ....

    (c) Write 0.15 as a fraction in its simplest form.   [2]

    ....

2. Which average is affected most by an outlier?   [1]

    ....

3. A bag contains three green counters, two blue counters and one white counter.
A counter is taken at random.

Draw and label arrows on the probability scale to show the probability of:

- Picking a green counter (G)

- Picking a blue counter (B)

- Picking a pink counter (P)   **[2]**

4. Dorcas is thinking of a number. She multiplies it by 4 and then adds 3. She gets the answer −5.

What number was she thinking of?   **[2]**

5. The results of a survey on the lifetime (in hours) of two different light bulbs are shown in the table.

	Magnabulb	Lighthouse Bulbs
Estimated mean	355	380
Median	340	365
Range	88	132

(a) Give one reason why Lighthouse Bulbs might be better.   **[1]**

(b) Give one reason why Magnabulb might be better.   **[1]**

6. Write down all the factors of 40. [2]

....

7. **(a)** Write down the value of 3^3. [1]

....

(b) Write down the value of 10^4. [1]

....

(c) Write down the value of $\sqrt[3]{8}$. [1]

....

8. Work out

$$\frac{3}{5} + \frac{1}{4}$$ [2]

....

9. George, Timmy and Ann shared some money in the ratio 5 : 7 : 9

Ann got £32 more than Timmy.

How much money did George get? [3]

£ ....

10. Jenni plays violin in an orchestra. She has 22 performances this year. For each performance she needs to get a return train ticket which costs £8.85. The orchestra pays $\frac{1}{4}$ of her travel costs.

(a) Estimate how much Jenni will have to pay in travel costs for the year.   [2]

£ ....

(b) Calculate the exact cost of the train tickets for the year.   [2]

£ ....

11. Solve the simultaneous equations $4x + y = 1$ [4]
$2x - y = 5$

$x =$ .... $y =$ ....

12. There are some orange and mint chocolates in a bag.

The probability of taking a mint chocolate is $\frac{1}{3}$

Amorreane takes a mint chocolate at random and eats it.

The probability of taking a mint chocolate is now $\frac{1}{4}$

How many orange chocolates are in the bag? [2]

....

13. Increase £340 by 15% [2]

....

14. A fair four-sided dice has the following coloured sides – blue, green, white and red.

The dice is rolled twice.

Complete the table to show all of the possible outcomes. [2]

		Second roll			
		Blue	**Green**	**White**	**Red**
First roll	**Blue**	B, B	B, G		
	Green	G, B			
	White				
	Red				

15. Ketsia starts with the number 3. She takes away a and then multiplies by b.

She gets an answer of 28. a is a negative integer and b is a positive integer.

Find two possible pairs of values for a and b. [2]

$a =$ .... $b =$ ....

$a =$ .... $b =$ ....

16. Work out

$$\frac{5}{8} \div \frac{2}{3}$$ [1]

....

17.

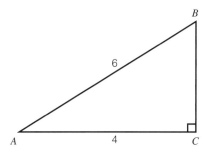

(a) Write down the value of cos A.　　　　　　　　　　　　　　　　　　　　**[1]**

....

(b) Calculate the length of BC. Leave your answer as a square root.　　　　**[3]**

....

18. Solve the equation $(x+1)(x-9)=0$　　　　　　　　　　　　　　　　　　　**[2]**

$x =$ .... or $x =$ ....

19. Alfred is 14 years old, Bertha is 15 and Cedric is 21. Every year they share £1400 in the ratio of their ages.

(a) How much money does Bertha get this year?　　　　　　　　　　　　　　**[2]**

....

(b) Does Cedric get more or less in two years' time? Show working to support your answer.　　**[3]**

....

20. Simplify $\left(3x^2y^5\right)^2$ [2]

....

21. The total TV sales over a five-year period for a national electrical store were 120 000 units.

Find the sales figures for computers and TVs in year 4. [3]

Year	Computer sales (thousands)	TV sales (thousands)
1	12	
2	14	
3	13	
4	a	$2a + 5$
5	16	

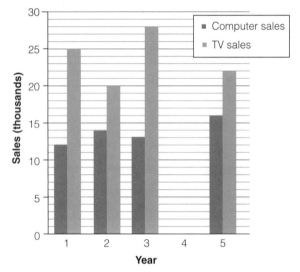

TV sales: ....

Computer sales: ....

22. Find the equation of the line that is parallel to $y = 2x + 7$ and passes through the point (0, –3). [2]

....

23. Here is a square and an isosceles triangle.

The length of each of the equal sides of the triangle is 3cm greater than the side of the square.

(a) If the perimeters of the two shapes are equal, find the value of x. **[3]**

(b) Show that the height of the triangle is equal to the diagonal of the square. **[3]**

24. Calculate the circumference of this circle.

3cm

Leave your answer in terms of π. **[2]**

.... cm

25. Which is more, 15% of 260 or 18% of 210?

Show your working. **[3]**

....

26. The fastest land animal is the **cheetah**, which has a recorded speed of 75mph.

The **peregrine falcon** is the fastest bird, with a speed of 389km/h.

The fastest animal in the sea is the **black marlin**, which has a recorded speed of 36m/s.

Put the speeds of these animals in order, fastest first. 5 miles = 8 kilometres **[3]**

....

27. Two cones S and T have volumes of 240cm³ and 810cm³ respectively.

(a) Write the ratio of the volumes S : T in its simplest form. **[1]**

....

(b) What is the ratio of the heights S : T? **[1]**

....

(c) If the surface area of cone S is 180cm², what is the surface area of cone T? **[2]**

.... cm²

28. The diagram below shows the graph of $y = x^2 - 8x + 17$

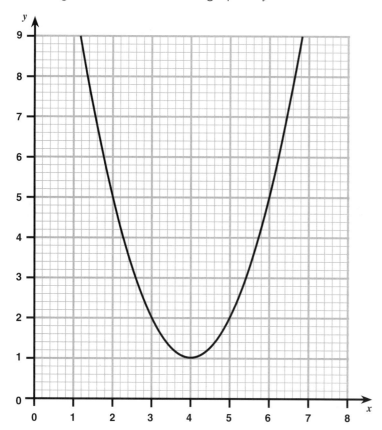

(a) Write down the equation of the line of symmetry. **[2]**

....

(b) Write down the coordinates of the turning point on the curve. **[2]**

....

(c) If the graph was extended, at which coordinates would it cross the y-axis? **[2]**

....

GCSE
Mathematics
Foundation tier

Paper 2   Time: 1 hour 30 minutes

For this paper you must have:

- a calculator
- mathematical instruments

Instructions

- Use black ink or black ball-point pen. Draw diagrams in pencil.
- Read each question carefully before you start to write your answer.
- Diagrams are not accurately drawn unless otherwise stated.
- Answer **all** the questions.
- Answer the questions in the space provided.
- In all calculations, show clearly how you work out your answer. Use a separate sheet of paper if needed. Marks may be given for a correct method even if the answer is wrong.
- If your calculator does not have a π button, take the value of π to be 3.142 unless the question instructs otherwise.

Information

- The mark for each question is shown in brackets.
- The maximum mark for this paper is 80.

Name: ....

1. Here are some numbers:

| 7 | 4 | 9 | 42 | 28 | 56 |

From this list of numbers write down:

(a) A multiple of 6 [1]

....

(b) A factor of 45 [1]

....

(c) A prime number [1]

....

2. Find the value of:

(a) 2.7^3 [1]

....

(b) $\sqrt{576}$ [1]

....

(c) $\sqrt[3]{9261}$ [1]

....

3. Match each speed–time graph, A, B and C, to the correct distance–time graph. **[2]**

A

B

C

1

2

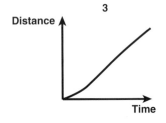

3

4. Lela is buying some new stationery. She buys:

- Three gel pens at £1.19 each
- Two erasers at 17p each
- Four pencils at 26p each
- A ruler at 45p

Lela pays with a £10 note.

How much change does she receive? **[3]**

5. Find two numbers, **greater than 71**, which have the following **two** properties:

- a multiple of 5 and 7
- a common factor of 420 and 630 **[4]**

6. Expand

(a) $6(x - 3)$ [2]

....

(b) $(x + 3)(x - 3)$ [2]

....

7. Calculate the area of this shape. Give your answer to 3 significant figures. [3]

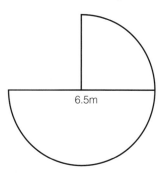

6.5m

....

8. A biologist conducted a survey of different lakes to investigate algae growth and the amounts
    of nitrate present. She recorded the concentrations of both algae and nitrate in a table.

Algae (cells/ml)	10	12	55	20	5	24	42	44	15	30	22	38
Nitrate (mg/L)	0.5	1.5	3.6	0.7	0.5	1.8	1.5	1.8	1.7	2.3	0.8	2.6

(a) Draw a scatter graph of this data on the grid below.   [2]

(b) What type of correlation is shown between nitrate levels and algae concentrations?   [1]

....

(c) Use the graph to estimate the nitrate levels in a lake with an algae concentration of 28 cells/ml.   [2]

                                                      .... mg/L

(d) The biologist wants to use this data to predict algae concentrations for any lake.

    Comment on the biologist's idea.   [1]

....

....

9. **(a)** Work out the following. Write down all the figures on your calculator display. [2]

$$\frac{\sqrt{35} + 6^2}{(2 - 0.04)^3}$$

....

(b) Round your answer in part (a) to 3 significant figures. [1]

....

10. Show that the point (−3, −2) lies on the curve $y = x^2 + 2x - 5$ [2]

....

....

....

....

11. Three feeding bowls, A, B and C, are placed in a cage with two hamsters. The hamsters are equally likely to choose any of the feeding bowls.

Find the probability that both hamsters choose bowl C. [2]

....

12. The following shape is made up of equilateral triangles.

Shade exactly $\frac{11}{16}$ of the shape. [2]

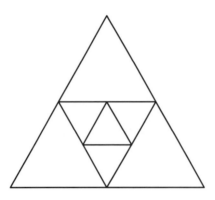

13. The distance from London to Manchester is 200 miles to the nearest 10 miles.

(a) What is the shortest possible distance, in miles, between London and Manchester? [1]

....

(b) Write down the error interval for the distance (d) between London and Manchester. [1]

....

14. The nth term in an arithmetic sequence is given by $U_n = 5n + 2$

Write down the first four terms in this sequence. [2]

....

15. Matthew is estimating the height of his house using the Sun.

A stick 1m long casts a shadow 60cm long. At the same time the shadow of the house is 5.4m long.

How tall is the house? **[3]**

....

16. Jerome is a salesman. He visits farms to try to sell gates and fencing equipment.

When Jerome visits a farm, the probability that he will make a sale is 0.4

One morning Jerome visits two farms.

(a) Complete the tree diagram to show all the outcomes. **[2]**

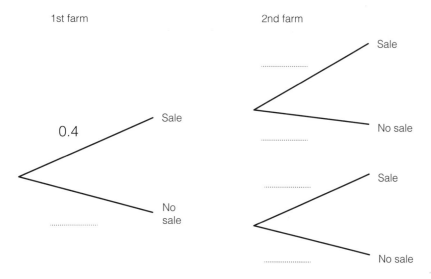

(b) Find the probability that Jerome sells equipment to at least one of the farms. **[2]**

....

17. The graph shows the temperature of a jug of custard as it cools.

Temperature change of custard

(a) Describe what happens in the first 5 minutes. [2]

....

....

....

....

(b) What is the temperature of the custard after 15 minutes? [1]

....

(c) What do you think happens between 20 and 30 minutes? [2]

....

....

....

....

18. Rearrange $y = \dfrac{10x - 2}{5 - x}$ to make x the subject. [4]

....

19. Calculate the surface area of this cylinder. Give your answer to 3 significant figures. **[3]**

75mm

5.2cm

.... cm²

20. Calculate the angle R. Give your answer to 3 significant figures. **[3]**

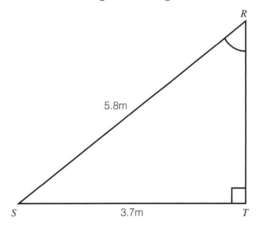

....

21. The ratio of the radii of two cones is 1 : 3

(a) Calculate the ratio of the curved surface areas of the cones. [1]

....

(b) If the volume of the larger cone is 10.8 litres, what is the volume of the smaller cone? [2]

....

22. Work out the equation of the line that is parallel to the line $y = 7 - 2x$ and passes through the point (8, −1). [4]

....

23. Copper and zinc are mixed to form an alloy in the ratio 9 : 7 by mass.

(a) If 27kg of copper are used to make a batch of alloy, how much alloy can be made? **[3]**

.... kg

(b) The density of copper is 8900kg/m³.

Find its density in g/cm³. **[4]**

.... g/cm³

24. Calculate angle *BCD*, giving your reasons. **[3]**

....

....

....

....

GCSE
Mathematics
Foundation tier

Paper 3   Time: 1 hour 30 minutes

For this paper you must have:
• a calculator   • mathematical instruments

Instructions

- Use black ink or black ball-point pen. Draw diagrams in pencil.
- Read each question carefully before you start to write your answer.
- Diagrams are not accurately drawn unless otherwise stated.
- Answer **all** the questions.
- Answer the questions in the space provided.
- In all calculations, show clearly how you work out your answer. Use a separate sheet of paper if needed. Marks may be given for a correct method even if the answer is wrong.
- If your calculator does not have a π button, take the value of π to be 3.142 unless the question instructs otherwise.

Information

- The mark for each question is shown in brackets.
- The maximum mark for this paper is 80.

Name:

1. Shade $\frac{2}{3}$ of this shape. [1]

2. Write the following numbers in order from smallest to largest.

(a) −5   3   7   −7   −3   0 [1]

....

(b) 0.39   0.33   0.03   0.3   0.309 [1]

....

3. (a) Round 345.934 to 2 significant figures. [1]

....

(b) Round 0.30492 to 3 significant figures. [1]

....

4. **(a)** Write the number 180 as a product of its prime factors. [2]

....

(b) Write your answer to part (a) in index form. [1]

....

5. Twenty-five pensioners are asked if they like tea or coffee. These are the responses:
    - 18 like tea
    - 19 like coffee
    - 4 like tea but not coffee

    Draw a Venn diagram to display these results. [3]

6. A restaurant has this special offer:

- £2.95 for a starter
- £6.50 for a main course
- £2.25 for a dessert

How much do two people pay in total if they each have three courses? [2]

£ ....

7. Water is poured into each of the containers A, B and C at a constant rate. The graphs show how the depth of water changes (y-axis) with time (x-axis).

Match each container with its correct graph. [2]

A

B

C

1

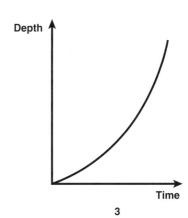
2

3

8. Lee weighs 89.3kg to the nearest 1 decimal place.

(a) What is the least amount that Lee could weigh? [1]

.... kg

(b) Write down the error interval for Lee's weight (W). [2]

....

9. A new tablet computer is released and the older model costing £425 is reduced by 12%.

What is its new price? [2]

£ ....

10. James pays £6 and Jamila pays £4 towards a raffle ticket. The ticket wins the star prize of £80.

If they share the money in the same ratio as they paid originally, how much more money does James get? [3]

....

11. Lyse and Lysette each test out a biased coin to find out the estimated probability of it landing on heads. Here are the results:

	Number of coin flips	Number of heads
Lyse	40	16
Lysette	80	28

(a) Whose results give the best estimate for the probability of getting heads?

Explain your answer. **[1]**

....

....

....

....

The coin is flipped 600 times.

(b) How many times do you expect the coin to land on heads? **[2]**

....

12. Find an integer value of x satisfying both $3x+4 > 19$ and $2x-1 < 13$ **[3]**

....

13. Sketch two graphs to show:

(a) y directly proportional to x. **[2]**

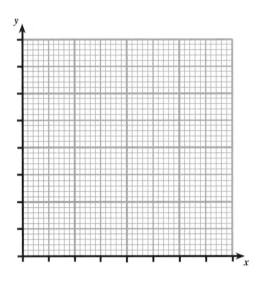

(b) y inversely proportional to x. **[2]**

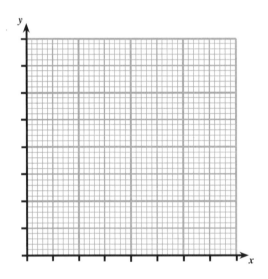

14. (a) Write $3^5 \div 3^{10}$ as a single power of 3. **[1]**

....

(b) Write 0.000 070 2 in standard form. **[1]**

....

(c) Calculate the value of 6^{-2} **[1]**

....

15. Here is a map of part of Norway.

Scale 1 : 6 500 000

(a) Estimate the straight-line distance from Trondheim to Bergen. [2]

....

(b) The actual road and ferry journey is 700km.

Express the road and ferry distance as a percentage of the straight-line distance. [2]

....

(c) If it takes 11 hours to make the journey by car, what is the average speed? [3]

....

16. A farmer measures the growth (measured as a change in height) of his crop over a period of eight weeks. The results are shown in the table below.

Growth (cm)	Frequency
$0 \leqslant h < 20$	11
$20 \leqslant h < 40$	38
$40 \leqslant h < 60$	49
$60 \leqslant h < 80$	30
$80 \leqslant h < 120$	12

(a) Which is the modal group? [1]

....

(b) Find the estimated mean growth for the crop over this period. [3]

.... cm

(c) The farmer says that over one-third of his crop grew by 60cm or more during this period.

Does the data support the farmer's claim? [2]

....

....

....

....

....

17. Using algebra, solve the equation $x^2 + 6x - 27 = 0$ [4]

....

18. The International Space Station (ISS) travels at a speed of 4.48×10^4 km/h.

(a) Write this value as an ordinary number. [1]

....

It takes three hours for the ISS to orbit the Earth twice.

(b) Find the distance that the ISS travels in one full orbit around the Earth.

Write your answer in standard form. [3]

....

19. Consider the function $f(x) = \dfrac{3x+9}{2}$

(a) Write down the outputs for each of the following inputs: [4]

Input x		**Output** $f(x)$
0	$\rightarrow$	....
1	$\rightarrow$	....
2	$\rightarrow$	....
3	$\rightarrow$	....

(b) Find the value of x that maps to itself. [2]

....

20.

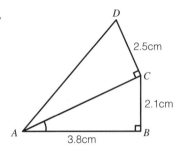

Find

(a) The size of angle CAB. [2]

....

(b) The area of triangle ACD. [4]

....

21. The value of a motorbike (£V) is given by the formula $V = 18\,000 \times 0.85^t$ where t is the age in whole number of years.

(a) What is the value of the bike when it is new? [1]

....

(b) What is the bike worth after two years? [2]

....

(c) After how many years will its value be below £10 000? [2]

....

22. Look at shape A on this grid.

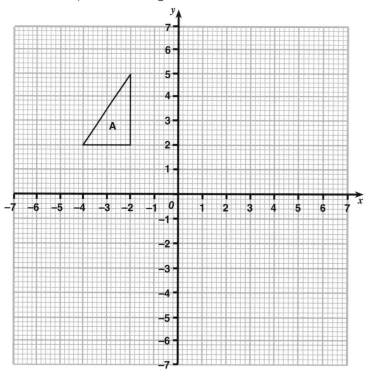

(a) Rotate shape A through 180° about centre (1, 0). Label the shape B. **[2]**

(b) Reflect shape B in the x-axis and label the new shape C. **[2]**

(c) Enlarge shape A, scale factor 2, centre (-6, 6). Label the enlarged shape D. **[2]**

Notes

You are encouraged to show your working out, as you may be awarded marks for method even if your final answer is wrong. Full marks can be awarded where a correct answer is given without working being shown but if a question asks for working out, you must show it to gain full marks. If you use a correct method that is not shown in the mark scheme below, you would still gain full credit for it.

Module 1: Place Value and Ordering

1. **(a)** −7   **(b)** 21   **(c)** −3

   Remember the rules for signs and BIDMAS.

2. **(a)** False   **(b)** True   **(c)** True   **(d)** False
3. **(a)** −3°C   **(b)** −9°C
4. **(a)** 5.418   **(b)** 5418   **(c)** 12 900   **(d)** 420

   Compare the position of decimal points with the original calculation.

5. **(a)** £35 **[Accept −£35]**
   (b) £35 − £14 **[1]** = £21 **[1] [Accept −£21]**

Module 2: Factors, Multiples and Primes

1. **(a)** 1 and 3   **(b)** 1, 4 and 16   **(c)** 6, 12, 24 and 48
2. 21 **[1]** or 45 **[1]**

   Test the prime numbers between 1 and 50.

3. **(a)** 55   **(b)** 7
4. **(a)** 72 = 2 × 2 × 18 = 2 × 2 × 2 × 3 × 3 **[2] [Two correct steps of decomposition get 1 mark]** = $2^3 \times 3^2$ **[1]**

   Use factor trees.

   (b) 90 = 2 × 3 × 15 **[1]** = 2 × 3 × 3 × 5 **[1]** = $2 \times 3^2 \times 5$ **[1]**
   (c) 2 × 3 × 3 **[1]** = 18 **[1]**

   Look for the common factors from the lists in (a) and (b).

   (d) 18 × 2 × 2 × 5 **[1]** = 360 **[1]**

   HCF × remaining factors.

5. Bus A: 12   24   36   48   60   72   84
   Bus B: 28   56   84   112   140   168   196 **[1]**
   LCM = 84 **[1]**
   8.00am + 84 minutes = 9.24am **[1]**

Module 3: Operations

1. **(a)** 17

   Multiplication before addition.

   (b) $\dfrac{3}{5}$

   (c) $\dfrac{1}{4}$

2. $\dfrac{(2)^2}{2}$ **[1]** = 2 **[1]**

3. **(a)** $\dfrac{12}{40}$ **[1]** = $\dfrac{3}{10}$ **[1]**   **(b)** $\dfrac{50}{18}$ **[1]** = $2\dfrac{7}{9}$ **[1]**

   Find the reciprocal of the second fraction and multiply.

   (c) $\dfrac{15-12}{20}$ **[1]** = $\dfrac{3}{20}$ **[1]**   **(d)** $\dfrac{9+5}{15}$ **[1]** = $\dfrac{14}{15}$ **[1]**

   Find a common denominator.

4. $1 - \left(\dfrac{2}{5} + \dfrac{3}{7}\right)$ **[1]** = $1 - \dfrac{29}{35}$ **[1]** = $\dfrac{6}{35}$ **[1]**
5. $1\dfrac{1}{4} \times 2\dfrac{2}{3}$ **[1]** = $\dfrac{5}{4} \times \dfrac{8}{3}$ **[1]** = $\dfrac{40}{12}$ = $3\dfrac{1}{3}$m² **[1]**
6. $1 - \left(\dfrac{3}{5} + \dfrac{2}{9}\right)$ **[1]** = $1 - \dfrac{37}{45}$ **[1]** = $\dfrac{8}{45}$ **[1]**

Module 4: Powers and Roots

1. **(a)** 3^6 **(b)** 12^4
2. $\sqrt[3]{64}$ $\sqrt[4]{625}$ 5^2 3^3 2^5
3. **(a)** $x = 7$ **(b)** $x = 125$ **(c)** $x = 3$

4. **(a)** 4^2

   Subtract the powers, i.e. 4^{6-4}

   (b) 5^{-2}
   (c) 0.0003

   The digits have moved four places.

5. **(a) (i)** 3.21×10^5 **(ii)** 6.05×10^{-4}
   (b) (i) 30×10^{-5} **[1]** = 3×10^{-4} **[1]**
       (ii) 41 000 + 3400 = 44 400 **[1]** = 4.44×10^4 **[1]**

6. **(a)** 1   **(b)** $\dfrac{1}{4^2} = \dfrac{1}{16}$

Module 5: Fractions, Decimals and Percentages

1. **(a)** 0.7
   (b) 0.75
   (c) 0.36

2. $\dfrac{17}{51}$ $\dfrac{3}{8}$ 0.475 $\dfrac{12}{25}$

   Convert all the values to decimals to compare them.

3. $\dfrac{56}{100} = \dfrac{14}{25}$

4. 5 ÷ 8 = 0.625 **[1]**   7 ÷ 11 = 0.6363... **[1]**

   $\dfrac{7}{11}$ is closer to $\dfrac{2}{3}$ (as $\dfrac{2}{3}$ = 0.6666...) **[1]**

5. **(a)** 37 × 49 = 1813 **[1]**
   So 3.7 × 4.9 = 18.13 **[1]**
   (b) 560 ÷ 14 **[1]** = 40
   So 56 ÷ 1.4 = 40 **[1]**

6. 34 × 129 **[1]** = 4386 **[1]**
   So total cost is £43.86 **[1]**

   Use long multiplication.

7. 0.2222...

   Use long division.

Module 6: Approximations

1. **(a)** 3500   **(b)** 29   **(c)** 700
2. **(a)** 9.49   **(b)** 6.554   **(c)** 5.60

   Use a calculator first.

3. **(a)** 400 000   **(b)** 0.0497   **(c)** 3.142

   Use a calculator to find π.

4. $\dfrac{20 \times 3}{0.5} = \dfrac{60}{0.5} = 120$ **[2]**
   [1 mark for rounding at least one number to 1 s.f.]
5. 500 ÷ 34 **[1]** = 14.7g **[1]**
6. 70 × 40 × 60 **[1]** = 168 000 **[1]**
   £1680 **[1]**
7. 1.65m **[1]** ≤ x <1.75m **[1]**

   0.05 above and below 1.7

Module 7: Answers Using Technology

1. **(a)** 410.0625   **(b)** 7   **(c)** 5
2. **(a)** $\dfrac{19.21}{32.76}$ **[1]** = 0.586 385 836 **[1]**

   (b) $\sqrt{28.8}$ **[1]** = 5.366 563 146 **[1]**

   Do not round at any point.

3. **(a)** 1.715×10^8 **(b)** 1.2×10^5

4. **(a)** $2\dfrac{20}{21}$

   Your calculator might show   2⌐20⌐21

Answers (vertical side tab)

(b) $31\frac{1}{18}$

5. **(a)** $1.496 \times 10^8 \div 400$ **[1]** $= 374\,000$ **[1]** $= 3.74 \times 10^5$ km **[1]**
   (b) $1.392 \times 10^6 \div 3.48 \times 10^3$ **[1]** $= 400$ **[1]** $= 4 \times 10^2$ **[1]**

Module 8: Algebraic Notation

1. **(a)** $5a+2$ **(b)** $15h+2k$ **(c)** $-2a+2b$ **(d)** $8x^2 - x + 1$

2. **(a)** $6p^7$ **(b)** $27p^{12}$ **(c)** $6f^5g$ **(d)** $\dfrac{1}{8p^6}$

3. **(a)** $12k^2$ **(b)** a^3 **(c)** $p^{\frac{5}{2}}$

   (d) $p^{\frac{13}{2}}$ or $\sqrt{p^{13}}$

4. **(a)** $\dfrac{1}{4}$ **(b)** $\dfrac{25}{4}$

   (c) 4 **(d)** 1

5. **(a)** Equation   **(b)** Identity   **(c)** Identity

   (d) Equation   **(e)** Equation

Module 9: Algebraic Expressions

1. **(a)** $6a - 12$ **[2]**
   (b) $3m^2 + 6m$ **[2]**
   (c) $8n^2 - 4np$ **[2]**
   (d) $8d + 2$ **[2]**
   (e) $4x + 22$ **[2]**
   > Remember in the last bracket, $-2 \times -3 = +6$

2. **(a)** $a^2 + 3a + 2a + 6$ **[1]** $= a^2 + 5a + 6$ **[1]**
   (b) $f^2 + 6f - 5f - 30$ **[1]** $= f^2 + f - 30$ **[1]**
   (c) $x^2 - 5x - 7x + 35$ **[1]** $= x^2 - 12x + 35$ **[1]**
   (d) $a^2 + 4a + 4a + 16$ **[1]** $= a^2 + 8a + 16$ **[1]**
   > Remember $(a + 4)^2$ means $(a + 4)(a + 4)$, **not** $a^2 + 16$
   (e) $a^2 - 9a - 9a + 81$ **[1]** $= a^2 - 18a + 81$ **[1]**

3. **(a)** $3(a - b)$ **[2]**
   (b) $2(3p + 4)$ **[2]**
   (c) $x(x - 7)$ **[2]**
   (d) $2q(p - 3)$ **[2]**
   (e) $5p(p - 2)$ **[2]**

4. $6x - 3 + 4x + 32 + 5$ **[1]** $= 10x + 34$ **[1]** $= 2(5x + 17)$ **[1]**

5. **(a)** $(p + 3)(p + 1)$ **[2]**
   (b) $(x - 3)(x - 7)$ **[2]**
   (c) $(a + 11)(a + 1)$ **[2]**
   (d) $(x + 3)(x - 4)$ **[2]**

6. **(a)** $(t + 3)(t - 3)$ **[2]**
   (b) $(4 + f)(4 - f)$ **[2]**
   (c) $(1 + 5n)(1 - 5n)$ **[2]**
   (d) $(t + 5)(t - 5)$ **[2]**
   (e) $(p^4 + 2)(p^4 - 2)$ **[2]**

Module 10: Algebraic Formulae

1. **(a)** 36 **(b)** -8 **(c)** 8

   (d) -5 **(e)** 6

2. $v - u = at$ **[1]**
   $a = \dfrac{v - u}{t}$ **[1]**

3. $5y = 2 + x$ **[1]**
   $x = 5y - 2$ **[1]**

4. $xy - 8y = 2 + 3x$ **[1]**
   $xy - 3x = 2 + 8y$
   $x(y - 3) = 2 + 8y$ **[1]**
   $x = \dfrac{2 + 8y}{y - 3}$ **[1]**

5. $q = r - p$ **[2]**
   > Try to write the given information mathematically first. This question is basically telling you that $p + q = r$, then asking you to rearrange the equation.

6. **(a)** 31.1 degrees Celsius (1 d.p.)
   (b) $9T_C = 5T_F - 160$ **[1]**
   $T_F = \dfrac{9T_C}{5} + 32$ **[1]**
   (c) 140 degrees Fahrenheit

Module 11: Algebraic Equations

1. $4x = 36$ **[1]**
   $x = 9$ **[1]**

2. $5x - 10 - 3x + 12 = 4$ **[1]**
   $2x = 2$
   $x = 1$ **[1]**

3. $3(x + 4) = 5(x - 2)$ **[1]**
   > You can 'cross multiply' by 3 and 5 to clear the fraction here.
   $3x + 12 = 5x - 10$ **[1]**
   $2x = 22$
   $x = 11$ **[1]**

4. $(x + 9)(x + 4) = 0$ **[1]**
   $x = -9$ or $x = -4$ **[2]**

5. $(x - 7)(x + 4) = 0$ **[1]**
   $x = 7$ or $x = -4$ **[2]**

6. $(4x - 3y = 14$ and$)$ $3x + 3y = 21$ **[1]**
   $7x = 35$ **[1]**
   $x = 5$ **[1]**
   $y = 2$ **[1]**

7. $8x + 4y = 20$ (and $3x + 4y = 10$) **[1]**
   $5x = 10$ **[1]**
   $x = 2$ **[1]**
   $y = 1$ **[1]**

8. **(a)** $x = 0.7$, $x = 6.3$ **[2]**
   (b) $x = -0.5$, $x = 7.5$ **[2]**
   > Remember to start with the equation you are trying to solve, i.e. $x^2 - 7x - 4 = 0$. You then get to $x^2 - 7x + 4$ by adding 8 to both sides of the equation. So draw the line $y = 8$ and see where the curve crosses.

Module 12: Algebraic Inequalities

1. $7x > 35$ **[1]**
   $x > 5$ **[1]**

2. $-3x \geqslant 3$ **[1]**
   $x \leqslant -1$ **[1]**

3. $38 > -2x$ **[1]**
   $-19 < x$ **[1]**
   $x > -19$ **[1]**

4. **(a)** $x \leqslant -1$ **(b)** $x > 3$ **(c)** $-4 \leqslant x < 2$

5. $x = -1, 0, 1, 2, 3, 4$ **[2]**

6. $x = -7, -6, -5, -4$ **[2]**

7. $x = 2, 3, 4, 5, 6$ **[2]**

8. $5 < 10x$ **[1]**
   $\dfrac{1}{2} < x$ $x > \dfrac{1}{2}$ **[1]**
   > Always rewrite your answer so it starts with 'x...'

[1]

9. $2x - 3 > 5$
   $2x > 8$ **[1]**
   $x > 4$ **[1]**
   AND
   $12 - x > 6$

$-x > -6$ **[1]**

$x < 6$ **[1]**

So $x = 5$ **[1]**

10. $x = 4, 5, 6, 7, 8, 9, 10, 11$ **[2]**

Module 13: Sequences
1. 24, 28 **[1 for each correct term]**
2. 5, -4 **[1 for each correct term]**
3. 1, 3, 13, 63, 313 **[2 if fully correct; 1 if one error]**
4. 8, 17, 26, 35 **[2 if fully correct; 1 if one error]**
5. **(a)** $U_n = 4n + 7$ **[1 for 4n; 1 for 7]**
   (b) Yes **[1]** since there is a whole number solution to $4n + 7 = 303$
   ($n = 74$) **[1]**
6. **(a)** $a = 15, d = 2$ **[2]**
   (b) $U_n = 2n + 13$ **[2]**
7. $\dfrac{1}{3}, \dfrac{1}{9}, \dfrac{1}{27}, \dfrac{1}{81}$ **[4]**

Module 14: Coordinates and Linear Functions
1. Line A: 6 **[1]**   Line B: -3 **[1]**   Line C: $\dfrac{-2}{3}$ **[1]**   Line D: 1 **[1]**
2. Lines A and C are parallel. **[2]**

> Rearrange each equation to make y the subject. You can then see clearly what the gradient is.

3. $x = 0$
4. $y = -6x + 9$ **[2]**

> You are told m and c in the question, so you can write the answer straight down by substituting these values into $y = mx + c$

5. $y = 5x + c$ **[1]**
   $1 = -15 + c$ **[1]**
   $c = 16$ **[1]**
   $y = 5x + 16$
6.

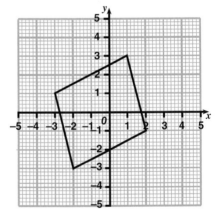

First three vertices plotted correctly **[1]**
Fourth vertex at $(-2, -3)$ **[2]**

7. $m = \dfrac{-5 - (-10)}{6 - (-4)}$ **[1]**

$m = \dfrac{1}{2}$

$y = \dfrac{1}{2}x + c$ **[1]**

Substitute in one coordinate to give $c = -8$ **[1]**

$y = \dfrac{1}{2}x - 8$ **[1]**

> Always show your working out for the gradient. Even if the final answer is wrong, you will still pick up some marks.

Module 15: Quadratic Functions
1. **(a)** $x = -5, x = 3$ **[2]**

> The roots will be where the curve crosses the x-axis.

   (b) $(0, -15)$ **[1]**
   (c) $(-1, -16)$ **[2]**

2. $(x + 4)(x - 11) = 0$ **[1]**
   $x + 4 = 0$ or $x - 11 = 0$
   $x = -4$ **[1]** or $x = 11$ **[1]**
3. **(a)** $x = -1.4, x = 3.4$ (or $x = -1.5, x = 3.5$) **[2]**
   (b) $(0, 5)$ **[1]**
   (c) $x = 1$ **[2]**
4. **(a)** $x = 4$ **[2]**

> Use $x = \dfrac{-b}{2a}$ for the line of symmetry when you don't have the curve.

   (b) $(4, -13)$ **[2]**

Module 16: Other Functions
1. 0 $\rightarrow$ 5 **[1]**
   1 $\rightarrow$ 17 **[1]**
   2 $\rightarrow$ 29 **[1]**

2. $f(x) = 3x - 3$ **[2]**
3. $x = 5, 6, 7$ **[3]**

> To find the first 'input' you just solve the equation $\dfrac{x + 3}{2} = 4$

4. **(a)** **(i)** General shape **[1]** going through origin. **[1]**
       (ii) Two parts **[1]** both not crossing axes. **[1]**

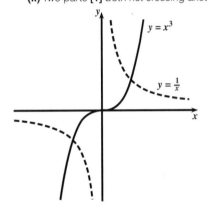

> When sketching two graphs on the same axes, make sure they cross in (approximately) the right place.

   (b) 2
5. Line 1: $y = x^2 - x^3$ **[1]**
   Line 2: $y = x$ **[1]**
   Line 3: $y = x^2 - x$ **[1]**
   Line 4: $y = -\dfrac{2}{x}$ **[1]**
6.

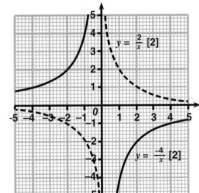

$y = \dfrac{2}{x}$ **[2]**

$y = \dfrac{-4}{x}$ **[2]**

Module 17: Problems and Graphs
1. **(a)** 11.30am
   (b) $1\dfrac{1}{2}$ hours

(c) $\dfrac{6}{1.5}$ **[1]** = 4km/h **[1]**

2. **(a)** $\dfrac{30}{10}$ **[1]** = 3m/s² **[1]**

   (b) 5 + 10 = 15s

   (c) $\left(\dfrac{1}{2} \times 10 \times 30\right)$ + (5 × 30) **[1]** = 150 + 150 = 300m **[1]**

3. **(a)** £3

   > The standing charge is the cost of getting into the taxi before actually travelling any distance.

   (b) £7.50

   (c) $\dfrac{6}{8}$ **[1]**

   $= \dfrac{3}{4}$ of £1

   = 75p **[1]**

   > The cost per mile is the gradient. As this is a straight line, it will not matter which two points you choose to calculate the gradient.

Module 18: Converting Measurements

1. 0.85 × 1.25 (or 850 × 1250) **[1]**
   = 1.06m² (3 s.f.) (or 1 062 500mm²) **[1]**
2. 3.4 × 1000² **[1]** = 3 400 000m² **[1]**
3. 100 × 100 × 100cm³ = 1m³ **[1]**
   1 000 000g = 1000kg **[1]**
4. 68 ÷ 5 × 8 or 110 ÷ 8 × 5 **[1]**
   108.8 or 68.75
   110km/h is faster **[1]**
5. 24 × 60 × 60m/hour **[1]** ÷ 1000 **[1]** = 86.4km/h **[1]**

   > Multiply m/s by 60 × 60 to convert to m/hr.

6. **(a)** Bob 626 ÷ 35 = £17.89/h **[1]**
      Leila 30 000 ÷ (32 × 52) **[1]** = £18.03/h
      Shahida has best hourly rate. **[1]**
   (b) Shahida 18.4 × 30 × 52 = £28 704
      Bob 626 × 52 = £32 552
      [1 for either Bob or Shahida correct]
      Bob earns most per year. **[1]**

      > 1 year = 52 weeks

7. **(a)** 463 ÷ 24 **[1]** = 19.29g/cm³ (2 d.p.) **[1]**
   (b) 19.29... × 30 **[1]** = 578.75g **[1]**
   (c) (463 + 578.75) × 23.50 **[1]** = £24 481.13 **[1]**
      [No mark for 24 481.125]

Module 19: Scales, Diagrams and Maps

1. **(a)** 3 × 20 = 60m
   (b) 57 ÷ 20 **[1]** = 2.85m **[1]**

   > Scale 1 : n means 1 and n given in cm. Convert n to m or km as necessary.

2. **(a)** 5.3cm to 5.5cm
   (b) 5.3 × 5 000 000 **[1]** = 265km **[1] [Accept up to 275km for a 5.5cm measurement]**
   (c) 203° (±3°) **[2]**
      [1 mark for correct construction or 157°]
   (d) (203) − 180 OR (203) + 180 − 360 **[1]** = 023° **[1]**
3. **(a)**

   [1 for correct drawing; 1 for accuracy]

(b) 318° (±3°) **[1]**
   58km (±2km) **[1]**

   > All bearings are measured clockwise from the North line.

4. **(a)** 18 × 25 000 **[1]** = 450 000cm = 4.5km **[1]**
   (b) **[2]**

   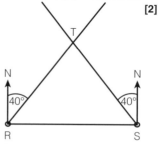

   [1 for one bearing correct]

Module 20: Comparing Quantities

1. 37.5%　　　$\dfrac{14}{5}$　　　$3\dfrac{5}{8}$

   [2 if fully correct; 1 for two correct]
2. 20%　　　0.21　　　0.211　　　$\dfrac{2}{9}$　　　$\dfrac{3}{10}$

   [2 if fully correct; 1 for four in correct order]

   > Change all amounts to decimals to find the correct order.

3. 2.8 − 2.5 = 0.3
   2.5 − 2.125 = 0.375 **[1]**
   0.3 < 0.375 so $2\dfrac{4}{5}$ closer **[1] [or equivalent working in fractions]**
4. $\dfrac{3}{8} \times \dfrac{5}{6}$ **[1]** $= \dfrac{5}{16}$ = 31.25% **[1]**

   OR $\dfrac{5}{6}$ of 12 = 10 **[1]**

   $\dfrac{10}{32}$ = 31.25% **[1]**
5. **(a)** 2.54 ÷ 3.45 OR 5.99 ÷ 3.45 **[1]** → 73.6% (1 d.p.) **[1]**
   (b) 3.45 × 1.15 **[1]** (= £3.97)
      (3.45 × 1.15) × 80 **[1]** (= £317.40)
      55 × 6.99 + 25 × 4 **[1]** = £484.45
      £484.45 − £317.40 = £167.05
      167.05 ÷ 317.40 = 52.6% **[1]**

      > Percentage profit = (profit ÷ original amount) × 100

6. **(a)** 0.4 × 0.55 **[1]** + 0.65 × (1 − 0.55) **[1]** = 51.25% **[1]**
   (b) $\dfrac{35}{100}$ **[1]** $= \dfrac{7}{20}$ **[1]**

Module 21: Ratio

1. 20cm : 3m **[1]** simplifies to 2 : 30 **[1]** All the rest simplify to 2 : 3

   > Divide all parts of the ratio by a common factor.

2. **(a)** 1 + 2 + 7 **[1]** = 10
      2 litres ÷ 10 **[1]** = 200ml
      Navy blue: 200ml; Grey: 400ml; White: 1400ml **[1]**
   (b) 1200 ÷ 2 = 600ml and 6000 ÷ 7 = 857ml so grey is limiting colour **[1]**
      1 lot is 600ml so total 600 × 10 = 6000ml = 6 litres **[1]**
3. A is $\dfrac{5}{8}$ of B
4. **(a)** 50 ÷ 5 = 10 so 3 biscuits need 10g.
      3 × 7 = 21 biscuits
      [1 for any correct method; 1 for correct answer]
   (b) 175 ÷ 5 = 35 so 35g flour for 3 biscuits.
      35 × 4 = 140g
      [1 for any correct method; 1 for correct answer]
5. No
   Blue costs 30 ÷ 5 **[1]** = £6/litre and yellow 28 ÷ 7 = £4/litre
   Cost for 7 litres 5 × 4 + 2 × 6 **[1]** = £32
   Lucy gets £4.50 × 7 = £31.50. So she loses 50p **[1]**

Module 22: Proportion

1. 59×2.5 **[1]** $= 147.5$kcal **[1]**
2. **(a)** $500 \times 1.29 = $ €645
   (b) $(645 - 570) \div 1.33$ **[1]** $=$ £56.39 **[1]**

   Each £ receives €1.29 → multiply. Each €1.33 receives
   £1 → divide.

3. **(a)** $1360 \div 80$ **[1]** $= 17$ litres/cow
   $17 \times (80 + 25)$ **[1]** $= 1785$
   $1785 \times 365 \times 0.3$ **[1]** $=$ £195 457.50 **[1]**
   (b) $800 \div 105 = 7.6$ days
   [1 for any correct method; 1 for correct answer]

   6 tonnes is 800 cattle feeds.

4. Scale factor $\times 1.5$ **[1]**
   $PR = 6 \div 1.5$ **[1]** $= 4$cm
   $TU = 4.5 \times 1.5 = 6.75$cm
   [1 for both correct values]

   Scale factor $= \dfrac{9}{6} = 1.5$

5. **(a)** $\dfrac{270}{120}$ **[1]** $= \dfrac{9}{4}$
   (b) Scale factor for length $= \sqrt{\dfrac{9}{4}}$ **[1]** $= \dfrac{3}{2}$ **[1]**
   (c) Scale factor for volume $= \dfrac{27}{8}$ **[1]**
   Volume of P $= 2700 \div \dfrac{27}{8}$ **[1]** $= 800$cm³ **[1]**

Module 23: Rates of Change

1. **(a)** $10\,000 \times 1.02^4$ or other stepwise method **[1]**
   $=$ £10 824.32 **[1]**
   [1 for 10 000 $\times$ 1.02]
   (b) $10\,000 \times 1.15$ **[1]** $\times 1.06 \times 0.82 \times 1.01$ **[1]**
   $=$ £10 095.76 **[1]**

2. No **[1]**
   $6500 \times 1.03 = 6695$ so £195 is correct for first year but the money invested for year 2 is $6500 + 195$ so it will earn more interest **[1]**.
   Actual interest $= 6500 \times 1.03^3 - 6500 = $ £602.73 **[1]**

3. **(a)** 20cm **(b)** Between 4 and 8 minutes **(c)** $20 \div 4 = 5$cm/min

   Steepest gradient gives fastest speed.

4. **(a)** Line drawn from $t = 8$ to the curve **[1]**
   96m **[1]**
   (b) $210 \div 10$ **[1]** $= 21$m/s (±0.4m/s) **[1]**

Module 24: Constructions

1. **[1 for correct construction lines shown; 1 for accuracy]**

   Always leave your construction lines and arcs, the examiner needs to see them.

2. **[1 for width 3.5cm; 1 for accurate lengths and 90° angles]**
3. **[1 for correct construction; 1 (conditional on construction) for angle of 90° ($\pm2°$)]**
4.

   [1 for circle radius 1.5cm around tree; 1 for line 2cm from DC; 1 for correct area shaded]
5. **[1 for equilateral triangle used to construct 60°; 1 for construction of angle bisector; 1 (conditional on construction) for angle of 30° ($\pm2°$)]**

Module 25: Angles

1. For tessellation, the angles must sum to 360°.
   Internal angle of a regular pentagon $= 108°$
   $360 \div 108$ is not a whole number.
   [1 for 108°; 1 for written or diagrammatic explanation]
2. $180 - 135$ **[1]** $= 45$
   $360 \div 45 = 8$ **[1]**

   It is always the **external** angles that sum to 360°.

3. Internal angle of hexagon $= 120°$
   Internal angle of octagon $= 135°$
   [1 for one correct method]
   $360 - (120 + 135)$ **[1]** $= 105°$ **[1]**
4. Triangle ABC <u>isosceles</u>
   Angle $ACB = \underline{180 - 2 \times 70}$ **[1]** $= 40°$
   Angle $FCD = 40°$ (<u>vertically opposite angles are equal</u>)
   Angle $FED = 360 - (130 + 130 + 40) = 60°$ **[1]**
   (<u>angles in a quadrilateral sum to 360°</u>)
   [1 for all four underlined reasons]

   Give a reason for each step of your working.

5. e.g. $\angle BPQ = 65°$ (vertically opposite angles equal)
   $\angle PRQ = 180 - 120 = 60°$ (angles on straight line sum to 180°)
   $\angle CPR = 60°$ **[1]** (alternate angles are equal)
   [1 for any correct, complete reasons]

Module 26: Properties of 2D Shapes

1. A – equilateral, B – obtuse isosceles, C – obtuse scalene,
   D – right-angled isosceles, E – scalene
   [3 if fully correct; 2 if three correct; 1 if one correct]
2. $\angle QBC = c$ (alternate angles are equal) **[1]**
   $\angle PBA = a$ (alternate angles are equal) **[1]**
   $a + b + c = 180°$ (angle sum on straight line $= 180°$) **[1]**
   Therefore angles in a triangle sum to 180°.

   A proof must work for every possible value so you will need to use algebra.

3. All angles at centre are equal and $360 \div 8 = 45°$
   All triangles isosceles so base angle $= (180 - 45) \div 2$ **[1]** $= 67.5°$
   1 internal angle $= 2 \times 67.5$ **[1]** $= 135°$
   Total $= 135 \times 8 = 1080°$ **[1]**
4. kite
5. Internal angle of an octagon $= 135°$
   Internal angle of an equilateral triangle $= 60°$ **[1 for either 135 or 60]**
   Angles at a point $= 360°$ so $x = 360 - (135 + 90 + 60)$ **[1]** $= 75°$ **[1]**

Module 27: Congruence and Similarity

1. B and E

   Similar means all angles the same / pairs of sides in the same ratio.

2. G and I

   Congruent = same shape **and** size

3. **(a)** $\dfrac{12}{8}$ or $\dfrac{8}{12}$ or 1.5 **[1]**
   $6 \times 1.5 = 9$cm **[1]**
   (b) $10 \div 1.5$ **[1]** $= \dfrac{20}{3}$ or $6\dfrac{2}{3}$ or 6.67cm **[1]**
4. Yes, both right angled with sides 3, 4, 5cm **[1]**, so SSS (or RHS) **[1]**
5. No. **[1]**
   A comparison of ratio **[1]**
   $\dfrac{156}{85} = 1.835 \neq \dfrac{142}{75} = 1.893$ or $\dfrac{156}{142} = 1.096 \neq \dfrac{85}{75} = 1.133$ (3 d.p.) **[1]**

Module 28: Transformations

1. (a) Reflection [1] in $y = x + 1$ [1]
   (b) Reflection in $x = -1$ [2 if fully correct; 1 if line drawn only]

2. Enlargement [1], scale factor $\frac{1}{2}$ [1], centre (0, 0) [1]

   Write one fact for each mark.

3.
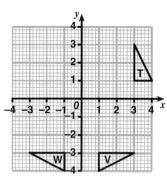

   (a) Correct plot
   (b) [2 if fully correct; 1 for rotation]

   Make sure you do the transformation on the correct shape.

   (c) [2 if fully correct; 1 for reflection of V if it was incorrect in part (b)]
   (d) Rotation, centre (0,0) [1],
       90° anti-clockwise **or**
       270° clockwise [1]

4.
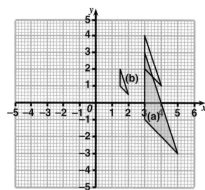

   (a) [2 if fully correct; 1 for correct scale factor × 2]
   (b) [2 if fully correct; 1 for correct scale factor × 0.5]

Module 29: Circles

1. (a) radius   (b) diameter
   (c) tangent   (d) circumference
   (e) arc   (f) sector
   (g) segment   (h) isosceles

2. $\pi \times 9$ [1] = 28.274... [1]
   = 28cm [1]

   Make sure you know (and use) the correct formula.

3. $\pi \times 4^2$ [1] = 16π [1] cm² [1]

   Here the diameter is given but you need the radius to work out area.

4. $\frac{\pi \times 5}{2} + 8 + \frac{\pi \times 5}{2} + 8$ (or equivalent) [1] = $5\pi + 16$
   = 31.7cm [1]

5. $\pi \times 10^2 \div 4$ [1] + $\pi \times 2.5^2$ = 98.174 777 [1] cm² [1]
   = 98.2cm² [1]

6. Radius of plane's journey is 6381 [1]
   $\pi \times 2 \times 6381 - \pi \times 2 \times 6370$ [1]
   or $2 \times \pi \times 11$ [1] = 69.1km [1]

Module 30: Properties of 3D Shapes

1. Pentagonal-based [1] pyramid [1]
2. A square-based pyramid [1] and triangular prism [1] accurately represented by diagrams [1]

3.
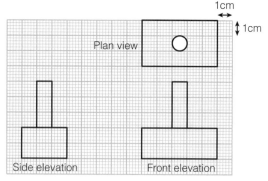

   [1 for each drawing; 1 for accuracy]

4.

   [3]

Module 31: Perimeter, Area and Volume

1. (a) Area: 8×3 [1] = 24m² [1]
       Perimeter: 26m [1]
   (b) Area: $\frac{1}{2} \times 14 \times 3$ [1] = 21cm² [1]
       Perimeter: 22.6cm [1]

2. $200 \times 80 - 25 \times 20$ [1] = 15500cm² [1] (or equivalent calculation to 1.55m²)

3. (a) $\frac{100 \times 80}{2}$ or $\frac{1 \times 0.8}{2}$ [1] = 4000cm² or 0.4m² [1]

   (b) $\frac{1}{2}(60 + 80) \times (100 - 75)$ or other correct method [1] = 1750cm² [1]

   (c) $\frac{75 \times 60}{2} - \pi \times 12.5^2$ [1] = 1759.126... cm² [1] = 1760cm² (3 s.f.)

4. $(\pi \times 4^2 \times 2)$ [1] + $(\pi \times 8 \times 5)$ [1] = $32\pi + 40\pi = 72\pi$cm² [1]

5. $3^3 + \frac{1}{3}\pi \times 1.5^2 \times 4$ [1] = 36.4 [1] cm³ [1]

6. $\frac{4}{3}\pi \times 3.5^3 = a^3$ [1]
   $a^3 = 179.59$ [1]
   $a = 5.64$cm (3 s.f.) [1]

7. $\frac{2}{3}\pi \times 5^3$ [1] = $\frac{250}{3}\pi$ [1] cm³ [1]

8. Surface area of cuboid $2 \times (4.4 \times 5.3 + 4.4 \times 1.8 + 5.3 \times 1.8)$ [1]
   = 81.6cm²
   Surface area of hemisphere $2\pi r^2 + \pi r^2$ [1] = $3 \times \pi \times 2.8^2$ [1]
   = 73.9cm²
   Cuboid larger [1 from correct values]

Module 32: Pythagoras' Theorem and Trigonometry

1. (a) $\cos p = \frac{2.8}{3.5}$ [1] = 0.8 [1]
       $p = 36.9°$ [1]
   (b) $\tan 51° = \frac{KL}{10.5}$ [1]
       $KL = 12.966$ [1] = 13.0m [1]

2. (a) $6^2 + NP^2 = 7^2$ [1]
       $NP = \sqrt{7^2 - 6^2} = 3.61$cm (3 s.f.) [1]
   (b) $\tan NOP = \frac{NP}{5.5}$ [1] = 0.6555
       Angle $NOP = \tan^{-1} 0.6555$ [1] = 33.2° (3 s.f.) [1]

3. $9^2 = 7^2 + q^2$ [1]

   Substitute the values in the Pythagoras equation and then rearrange it.

   $q^2 = 9^2 - 7^2$ [1] = 32
   $q = \sqrt{32}$ (or $4\sqrt{2}$) [1]

4. (a) (i) $\frac{1}{\sqrt{2}}$ or $\frac{\sqrt{2}}{2}$ (ii) 1

(b) $a = 2 \times \sin 60° = 2 \times \dfrac{\sqrt{3}}{2}$ **[1]** $= \sqrt{3}$ cm **[1]**

$\quad b = 2 \times \cos 60° = 2 \times \dfrac{1}{2}$ **[1]** $= 1$cm **[1]**

5. $\sin x = \dfrac{1}{5}$ **[1]**

$\quad x = \sin^{-1} \dfrac{1}{5}$ **[1]** $= 11.5°$ **[1]**

Module 33: Vectors

1. $\mathbf{a} = 2\mathbf{r}$ $\qquad\qquad \mathbf{b} = -3\mathbf{s}$

$\quad \mathbf{c} = \mathbf{r} + \mathbf{t}$ $\qquad\quad \mathbf{d} = 2\mathbf{t} - \mathbf{s}$ or $\mathbf{d} = \mathbf{r} + \mathbf{t} - 2\mathbf{s}$

$\quad$**[1 for each correct answer]**

2. (a) $\mathbf{b}$ $\qquad\qquad\qquad$ **(b)** $-\mathbf{b}$

$\quad$**(c)** $\mathbf{a} + \mathbf{c}$ $\qquad\qquad$ **(d)** $\mathbf{a} - \mathbf{b}$

$\quad$**(e)** $\mathbf{b} - \mathbf{a} - \mathbf{c}$ (or equivalent)

$\quad$**(f)** $\mathbf{c} + \mathbf{a} - \dfrac{1}{2}\mathbf{b}$ (or equivalent)

3. (a) $\overrightarrow{BE} = -2\mathbf{b}$

$\quad$**(b)** $\overrightarrow{AC} = \mathbf{b} + \mathbf{d}$ **[2]**

$\quad$**(c)** $\overrightarrow{CE} = \overrightarrow{CB} + \overrightarrow{BE} = -2\mathbf{b} - \mathbf{d}$ **[2]**

> The opposite sides of a parallelogram are described with equal vectors.

4. $\overrightarrow{OR} = 2\mathbf{q}$ **[1]**

$\quad \overrightarrow{PQ} = \mathbf{q} - \mathbf{p}$ **[1]**

$\quad \overrightarrow{PR} = 2\mathbf{q} - \mathbf{p}$ **[1]**

Module 34: Experimental and Theoretical Probability

1.

2. (a) $\dfrac{4}{14}$ or $\dfrac{2}{7}$ $\quad$ **(b)** $\dfrac{5}{14}$ $\quad$ **(c)** $\dfrac{9}{14}$

3. $1 - (0.2 + 0.3 + 0.25 + 0.1)$ **[1]** $= 0.15$ **[1]**

4. (a) $\dfrac{12}{25}$ or 0.48

$\quad$**(b)** $3 + 4 + 12 = 19$ **[1]**

$\quad \dfrac{19}{25} \times 250$ **[1]** $= 190$ **[1]**

Module 35: Representing Probability

1. (1, head), (1, tail), (2, head), (2, tail), (3, head), (3, tail), (4, head), (4, tail), (5, head), (5, tail), (6, head), (6, tail)

$\quad$**[2 for all 12 outcomes; 1 if one missing or repeated answers have been included]**

2. (a)

			Dice			
		1	**2**	**3**	**4**	**5**	**6**
Spinner	**1**	2	3	4	5	6	7
	3	4	5	6	7	8	9
	5	6	7	8	9	10	11

$\quad$**[2 if fully correct; 1 for two correct rows or four correct columns]**

$\quad$**(b)** $\dfrac{6}{18}$ or $\dfrac{1}{3}$ $\qquad$ **(c)** $\dfrac{9}{18}$ or $\dfrac{1}{2}$

> Only count the 18 outcomes, not the numbers on the dice and spinner.

3. (a)
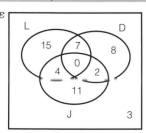

[3 if fully correct; 2 for six correct numbers; 1 for three correct numbers]

> 0 in the middle since no one can vote for all three. All the numbers in the diagram must add up to 50.

$\quad$**(b)** $\dfrac{11}{50}$

Module 36: Data and Averages

1. (a) 498 $\qquad\qquad$ **(b)** 499

> The median is between 498 and 500 and so is 499.

$\quad$**(c)** Any suitable answers, e.g. The sample size is too small. Need to sample across the range of times during production.

$\quad$**[1 for each reason up to a maximum of 2]**

2. (a) $60 \leqslant w < 80$

> Median value is between the 80th and 81st value, which is in the $60 \leqslant w < 80$ class interval.

$\quad$**(b)** Correct midpoints (35, 45, 55, 70, 90, 110, 135) **[1]**
$\quad$ Correct total of midpoint $\times$ frequency of 10 915 **[1]**
$\quad$ Estimated mean = 68.2g **[1]**

$\quad$**(c)** $20 + 25 + 22 + 44 = 111$ **[1]**
$\quad$ $111 \div 160 = 69.4\%$ **[1]**

3. 6, 6, 6, 7, 10 or 6, 6, 6, 8, 9 **[3]** Other solutions are possible.

$\quad$**[1 mark for any one of and 2 marks for any two of: a total of 35, median of 6 or mode of 6]**

> The total of all five numbers must be 35, i.e. 5 (cards) $\times$ 7 (mean) = 35

Module 37: Statistical Diagrams

1. (a) 21

$\quad$**(b)** A bar chart or vertical line graph, with frequency on the y-axis and days of the week on the x-axis, e.g.

$\quad$**[1 for selecting a dual bar chart or vertical line diagram; 1 for fully correct data (frequencies for each bars); 1 for a fully labelled chart]**

2. Biscuit Treats: 21 **[1]**
$\quad$ Meaty Sticks: 5 **[1]**
$\quad$ Sum to 60 **[1]**

> Place the known data into the Venn diagram starting with the overlap (buy both).

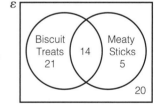

3. Table completed as follows:
$\quad$ Seafood – 106.7°; Meat – 66.7°;
$\quad$ Chicken – 53.3°; Mushroom – 55 and 73.3° **[1 for correct frequency of mushroom and 1 for correct angles]**

> Total frequency must be $45 \times 6 = 270$ as vegetarian represents one-sixth of the pie chart. $270 - 215 = 55$ mushroom

4. (a) Attempt to draw a graph to interpret the data **[1]**
$\quad$ Appropriate line of best fit drawn **[1]**
$\quad$ Estimate 175–195 million **[1]**

$\quad$**(b)** Any suitable answer, e.g. It would not be reliable to use the graph to predict sales in year 14 because it is beyond the range of the data **[1]** and the trend of sales may change **[1]**.

5. (a) A scatter graph drawn with age on x-axis and speed on y-axis **[1]** and the points correctly plotted **[1]**. Data supports John's conclusion. **[1]**

(b) Negative correlation

The trend shows that the younger the driver, the higher the speed; and the older the driver, the lower the speed. So the correlation is negative.

Module 38: Comparing Distributions

1.

	Represents a single value	Affected by outliers	Measure of spread
Mode	✓	✗	✗
Median	✓	✗	✗
Mean	✗	✓	✗
Range	✗	✓	✓

[2 if fully correct; 1 if one error]

2. Class A: Median 45, Mean 48.8 **[2]**

Class B: Median 42, Mean 45.7 **[2]**

Any suitable conclusion, e.g. Class A has a higher mean and a higher median; or Class B is more consistent **[1]**

Find the mean and median for the two groups of data and then compare.

3. (a) Mean will be higher as her distance is higher than current mean.

(b) The median may be higher as it's also higher than current median but you can't be certain without knowing the other values.

4. Calculation of estimated mean: £244 for 30–50 year olds and £329 for under 30s **[2]**

Median intervals of $200 \le c < 250$ for 30–50 year olds and $300 \le c < 350$ for under 30s **[1]**

[1 mark for a suitable comparison of the estimated means]

[1 mark for a suitable comparison of median intervals]

Practice Exam Paper 1

1. (a) 26

(b) 0.3

(c) $\dfrac{15}{100}$ **[1]** $= \dfrac{3}{20}$ **[1]**

2. Mean

3.

[2 for three correct; 1 for two correct]

4. $-5 - 3 = -8$ **[1]**

$-8 \div 4 = -2$ **[1]**

Work backwards

5. (a) Any suitable reasons, e.g. higher mean or median

(b) Performance more consistent (range 88 vs 132)

6. 1, 2, 4, 5, 8, 10, 20, 40

[2 if fully correct; 1 for 5–7 correct factors]

7. (a) 27

(b) 10 000

(c) 2

8. $\dfrac{12}{20} + \dfrac{5}{20}$ **[1]** $= \dfrac{17}{20}$ **[1]**

Find equivalent fractions with a common denominator.

9. Ann got two lots more than Timmy.

1 lot $\dfrac{£32}{2} = £16$ **[1 for showing correct division]**

George got (16) × 5 **[1 for your answer × 5]** = £80 **[1]**

Read the question carefully.

10. (a) $\left(\dfrac{20 \times 9}{4}\right) \times 3$ **[1]** = £135 **[1]**

Round each number to 1 significant figure.

(b) $885 \times 22 = 19\,470$ **[1]**

$8.85 \times 22 = £194.70$ **[1]**

Use long multiplication and count decimal places or use your own method.

11. Attempts to add both equations **[1]**

$6x = 6$ **[1]**

$x = 1$ **[1]**

$y = -3$ **[1]**

12. P(orange) $= \dfrac{2}{3}$ **[1]**

$\dfrac{2}{3}$ of 9 = 6 **[1]**

To start with there was a multiple of 3 chocolates and then a multiple of 4 after 1 had been eaten. So there must have been 9 chocolates to start with.

13. 10% = 34, so 5% = 17 **[1]**

$340 + 34 + 17 = £391$ **[1 for correct answer including units]**

14.

		Second roll			
		Blue	**Green**	**White**	**Red**
First roll	**Blue**	B, B	B, G	B, W	B, R
	Green	G, B	G, G	G, W	G, R
	White	W, B	W, G	W, W	W, R
	Red	R, B	R, G	R, W	R, R

[2 if fully correct; 1 for at least two columns or two rows correct]

15. $a = -1$ and $b = 7$, $a = -4$ and $b = 4$, $a = -11$ and $b = 2$, $a = -25$ and $b = 1$

[1 mark for each correct pair of answers]

Since a must be a negative number, the solution $a = 1$, $b = 14$ is invalid.

16. $\dfrac{15}{16}$

Turn the second fraction upside down and multiply.

17. (a) $\dfrac{4}{6}$ **[1]** $= \dfrac{2}{3}$

(b) $BC^2 + 4^2 = 6^2$ **[1 for correct use of Pythagoras]**

$BC = \sqrt{6^2 - 4^2}$ **[1]** $= \sqrt{20}$ **[1]**

18. $x = -1$ **[1]**

$x = 9$ **[1]**

19. (a) $1400 \div (14 + 15 + 21)$ **[1]** $= 28$

$28 \times 15 = £420$ **[1]**

(b) Less.

$1400 \div (16 + 17 + 23)$ **[1]** $= 25$

$(£25 \times 23) = £575$ **[1]** and $(£28 \times 21) = £588$ **[1]**

20. $9x^4 y^{10}$ **[2]**

21. Using the bar chart to find correct total of years

1, 2, 3, 5 = 95 **[1]**

TV sales: $120 - 95 = 25$ (i.e. 25 000) **[1]**

Computer sales: Solving $2a + 5 = 25$, so $a = 10$ (i.e. 10 000) **[1]**

22. $m = 2$, $c = -3$ **[1]**

$y = 2x - 3$ **[1]**

Gradients of parallel lines are equal.

23. (a) Sides of triangle $x + 3$ **[1]**

Perimeter of triangle = perimeter of square

$3x + 6 = 4x$ **[1]**

$x = 6$cm **[1]**

(b) Height of triangle $= \sqrt{9^2 - 3^2}$ **[1 for correct use of Pythagoras on half of triangle]** $= \sqrt{72}$ **[1]**

Diagonal of square $= \sqrt{6^2 + 6^2} = \sqrt{72}$ **[1]** Therefore equal.

24. $\pi \times 3 \times 2$ **[1]** $= 6\pi$cm **[1]**

25. 15% of 260 = 26 + 13 = 39 **[1]**

18% of 210 = 21 + 21 − 4.2 = 37.8 **[1 for any correct method]**

So 15% of 260 is greater **[1 for stating the correct answer]**

> In non-calculator percentage questions, there can be several ways to get the correct answer. Here 18% = 20% − 2% or 10% + 5% + 3%. Make sure your working is clear.

26. 75mph = 75 ÷ 5 × 8 = 120km/h **[1]**

36m/s = 36 ÷ 1000 × 60² **[1]** = 130km/h (sufficient accuracy for comparison)

Peregrine falcon; Marlin; Cheetah **[1]**

27. (a) 240 : 810 = 8 : 27

(b) $\sqrt[3]{8} : \sqrt[3]{27}$ = 2 : 3

(c) Ratio for area is 4 : 9 **[1]**

Surface area of B = $180 \times \dfrac{9}{4}$ = 405cm² **[1 for correct value]**

28. (a) $x = 4$ **[2]**

(b) (4, 1)   **[2]**

(c) (0, 17)   **[2]**

Practice Exam Paper 2

1. (a) 42   **(b)** 9   **(c)** 7

2. (a) 19.683   **(b)** 24   **(c)** 21

> Use the power and root buttons on a scientific calculator.

3. A2, B3, C1 **[2]**

[1 for one correct match]

> When the distance is increasing at a steady rate, the speed is constant.

4. 3 × 1.19 = £3.57

2 × 0.17 = £0.34

4 × 0.26 = £1.04 **[1]**

3.57 + 0.34 + 1.04 + 0.45 = £5.40 **[1]**

£10 − £5.40 = £4.60 **[1]**

5. 105 **[1]** and 210 **[1]**

420 = 2 × 2 × 3 × 5 × 7 **[1]**

630 = 2 × 3 × 3 × 5 × 7 **[1]**

> Use prime factor trees to find the two common factors 2 × 3 × 5 × 7 = 210 and 3 × 5 × 7 = 105

6. (a) 6x − 18 **[2]**   **(b)** $x^2 - 9$ **[2]**

7. π × 3.25² **[1]**

$\pi \times 3.25^2 \times \dfrac{3}{4}$ **[1]** = 24.887…

24.9m² **[1 for correct rounding and units]**

8. (a)

[2 if fully correct; 1 if one error]

(b) Weak positive

> The general trend is the greater the nitrate levels, the greater the algae concentration, but some of the results are still quite far apart.

(c) Correctly read from line of best fit as shown above **[1]**: range 1.6−1.9mg/L **[1]**

(d) Predictions will only be reliable within the range of the nitrate levels in this data (i.e. 0.5−3.6mg/L).

9. (a) $\dfrac{41.91607978}{7.529536}$ **[1]** = 5.566 887 49… **[1]**

> Work out the numerator and denominator separately and write them down.

(b) 5.57 (or your answer to part (a) correctly rounded)

10. −2 = (−3)² + 2(−3) − 5 **[1]**

−2 = 9 − 6 − 5

−2 = −2 **[1]**

> Substitute $x = -3$ and $y = -2$ into the equation. Remember negative integer rules.

11. $\dfrac{1}{3} \times \dfrac{1}{3}$ **[1]** = $\dfrac{1}{9}$ **[1]**

12. Any suitable answer, e.g.

[2 if fully correct; 1 for two medium triangles shaded plus one or two smaller triangles]

> Each of the larger triangles is worth $\dfrac{4}{16}$ of the whole shape.

13. (a) 195   **(b)** $195 \leqslant d < 205$

14. 7, 12, 17, 22 **[2]**

15. 60 : 100 = 3 : 5 **[1 for correct ratio]**

$5.4 \times \dfrac{5}{3}$ **[1]** = 9m **[1 for answer and units]**

> You may use another correct method, e.g. 60cm × 5.4 = 900cm = 9m

16. (a) First farm (no sale): 0.6 **[1]**

Second farm (from top to bottom): 0.4, 0.6, 0.4, 0.6 **[1]**

(b) 1 − (0.6 × 0.6) **[1]** = 1 − 0.36 = 0.64 **[1]**

> Calculate 1 − P(no sale, no sale)

17. (a) The temperature starts at 100°C and falls **[1]** to about 60°C **[1]**.

(b) Any answer in the range 22°C–25°C

(c) The curve levels out / the custard does not cool as quickly **[1]**. It stays at about 20°C / room temperature **[1]**.

18. $5y - xy = 10x - 2$ **[1]**

$5y + 2 = 10x + xy$ **[1]**

$5y + 2 = x(10 + y)$ **[1]**

$x = \dfrac{5y + 2}{10 + y}$ **[1]**

19. 2(π × 5.2²) **[1]** + 2 × π × 5.2 × 7.5 **[1]** = 414.941… cm²

= 415cm² **[1]**

20. $\sin R = \dfrac{3.7}{5.8}$ **[1]** = 0.6379…

$\sin^{-1} \dfrac{3.7}{5.8}$ = 39.6377… **[1]** = 39.6° **[1 for correct rounding and degree symbol]**

21. (a) 1 : 9

(b) 10 800 ÷ 27 **[1]** = 400ml (or 400cm³) **[1]**

22. $m = -2$ **[1]**

−1 = −2 × 8 + c **[1]**

c = 15 **[1]**

$y = -2x + 15$ **[1]**

23. (a) $\dfrac{27}{9}$ **[1]** = 3

9 + 7 = 16 **[1 for adding parts]**

3 × 16 = 48kg **[1]**

(b) 10⁶cm³ in 1m³ **[1]**

8900 × 1000g **[1]**

8900 × 1000 ÷ 1 000 000 **[1]** = 8.9g/cm³ **[1]**

24. ∠BAC = 50° **[1]** (alternate angles are equal)

∠BCA = 180 − (50 + 75) = 55° (angle sum of a triangle = 180°)

∠BCD = 180 − (55 + 80) = 45° (angles on a straight line = 180°)

[1 for correct answer; 1 for three correct reasons]

Practice Exam Paper 3

1. Any eight parts shaded.

2. (a) $-7, -5, -3, 0, 3, 7$
   (b) $0.03, 0.3, 0.309, 0.33, 0.39$

3. (a) 350
   (b) 0.305

   > The second zero is significant as it comes after the first significant figure.

4. (a) $180 = 2 \times 2 \times 45$ **[1]**
   $180 = 2 \times 2 \times 3 \times 3 \times 5$ **[1]**
   > Use prime factor trees.

   (b) $2^2 \times 3^2 \times 5$

5.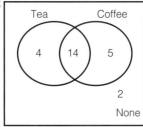

   [3 if fully correct; 2 if three numbers correct;
   1 if two numbers correct]

   > Make sure all the numbers sum to 25. The numbers inside 'Tea' should sum to 18 and the numbers inside 'Coffee' should sum to 19. If the three numbers in the circles don't add up to 25, then there must be some pensioners who don't like either.

6. $(2.95 + 6.50 + 2.25) \times 2$ **[1]**
   £23.40 **[1]**

7. A3, B2, C1 **[2]**
   [1 for one correct match]

8. (a) 89.25kg
   (b) $89.25\text{kg} \leq W < 89.35\text{kg}$ **[1]** [1 for correct symbols]
   > The error interval is half a decimal place above and below 89.3

9. $425 \times 0.88 = £374$
   [2 for correct answer; 1 for any correct method]
   > The multiplier method or working out 12% and subtracting are both correct. If you use a mental method on a calculator paper, you must get the answer correct to gain any marks.

10. $6 + 4 = 10$ or $3 : 2$ and $3 + 2 = 5$ **[1]**
    $\dfrac{80}{5}$ or $\dfrac{80}{10}$ **[1]**
    James £48, Jamila £32
    Difference £16 **[1]**

11. (a) Lysette, as she has done more coin flips.
    (b) $\dfrac{44}{120} \times 600$ **[1]** $= 220$ **[1]**
    > Use both of their results added together to get the best estimate.

12. $3x + 4 > 19 \Rightarrow x > 5$ **[1]**
    $2x - 1 < 13 \Rightarrow x < 7$ **[1]**
    So $x = 6$ **[1]**

13. (a)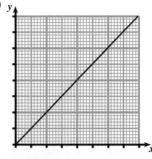
    [1 for straight line with positive gradient; 1 for line from (0, 0)]

    (b)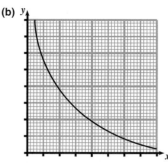
    [1 for concave curve; 1 for lines approaching but not touching axes]

14. (a) 3^{-5} (b) 7.02×10^{-5} (c) $\dfrac{1}{36}$ (or 0.0277...)
    > Remember the index rules.

15. (a) [1 for correct use of scale]
    Answer in range 420−450km **[1]**

    (b) Using your answer from part (a) (for example we are using 440km) $\dfrac{700}{440} = 1.590 = 159\%$ Answer in range 155−165%
    [1 for correct division; 1 for correct percentage]

    (c) $\dfrac{700}{11} = 63.64 = 64\text{kmh}^{-1}$ or 64km/h
    [1 for method; 1 for correct answer; 1 for correct unit]

16. (a) $40 \leq h < 60$
    (b) Midpoints (10, 30, 50, 70, 100) **[1]**
    Sum of frequency $\times$ Midpoints $= 7000$ **[1]**
    $7000 \div 140 = 50\text{cm}$ **[1]**
    (c) Correct calculation of $42 \div 140 = 30\%$ or $\dfrac{3}{10}$ **[1]**

    So the data does not support the farmer's claim. **[1]**

17. $(x + 9)(x - 3) = 0$ **[2]**
    $x = -9$ **[1]**
    $x = 3$ **[1]**

18. (a) 44 800km/h
    > There should be four digits after the first 4.

    (b) $(44\,800 \times 3) \div 2$ **[1]** $= 67\,200$ **[1]** $= 6.72 \times 10^4\text{km}$ **[1]**
    > Remember to put your answer back into standard form, with any relevant units.

19. (a) 4.5, 6, 7.5, 9 **[4]**
    (b) Attempt to solve $\dfrac{3x + 9}{2} = x$ **[1]**
    $x = -9$ **[1]**

20. (a) $\tan CAB = \dfrac{2.1}{3.8}$ **[1]** $= 0.5526....$
    $CAB = \tan^{-1}\dfrac{2.1}{3.8} = 28.9°$ **[1]** (3 s.f.)
    (b) $AC^2 = 3.8^2 + 2.1^2$ **[1]** $= 18.85$
    $AC = \sqrt{3.8^2 + 2.1^2} = 4.3416...$ **[1]** cm
    Area $= \dfrac{AC \times 2.5}{2}$ **[1]** $= 5.43\text{cm}^2$
    [1 including units but accept 5.427 or better]

21. (a) £18 000
    (b) $18\,000 \times 0.85 \times 0.85$ **[1]** $= £13\,005$ **[1]**
    (c) $18\,000 \times 0.85^4 = £9396.11$ **[1]**
    4 years **[1]**

22.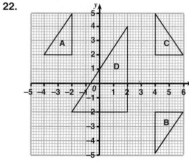
    (a) [2 if fully correct; 1 for correct size and orientation]
    (b) [2 if fully correct; 1 for correct size and orientation]
    (c) [2 if fully correct; 1 for correct size and orientation]